FLORENCE NIGHTINGALE

FLORENCE NIGHTINGALE

BY

ELSPETH HUXLEY

CHANCELLOR
PRESS

First published in Great Britain by Weidenfeld and Nicolson Ltd

This edition published by Chancellor Press
59 Grosvenor Street
London W1

ISBN 0 907486 20 7

Printed in Czechoslovakia
50482

For Mama – another indomitable nonagenarian

ACKNOWLEDGMENTS

The author is indebted to all the various writers who have undertaken research into the life of Florence Nightingale, and particularly to Mrs Cecil Woodham-Smith.

Photographs and illustrations were supplied by or reproduced by kind permission of the following:
Bettmann Archive Inc.: 197; British Museum: 100, 189 (photo John Freeman); Local History Collection, Swiss Cottage Library, Borough of Camden (photo C. Edwards & Son Ltd): 221; the Lt General Commanding Coldstream Guards, Chelsea Barracks (photo A. C. Cooper Ltd): 65; *Country Life*: 176, 176–7; John Frost Collection: 58, 247; John Freeman: 92; Greater London Council: 68, 206; The Nightingale Collection at the Greater London Record Office: 180–1, 193; Greater London Record Office: 185; *The Illustrated London News*: 48–9, 69 (top), 99, 121, 155, 158; India Office Library (photo R. B. Fleming): 200, 201, 202; Mansell Collection: 31, 32, 33, 187 (*left*), 239; National Army Museum: 63, 69 (*bottom*), 86–7, 89, 90–1, 93 (*top*), 93 (*bottom*), 94, 96, 112, 122–3, 130 (*left*), 130 (*right*), 134–5, 136–7; National Portrait Gallery: 26, 28, 52, 54, 66–7, 148–9, 167, 170, 199, 240; National Trust (photo John Bethell): 8–9, 10, 13, 25, 42, 51, 55, 126–7, 139, 232, 234–5, 242; National Trust (photo D. M. Nicholson): 231; Radio Times Hulton Picture Library: 12, 16, 18–19, 22, 36–7, 39, 57, 60–1, 64, 73, 74, 77, 82, 85, 102, 103, 105, 108, 111, 114–15, 116, 118–19, 125, 144–5, 152, 162, 169, 204, 210, 215, 218, 219, 225, 237 (*top*), 245; Ronan Picture Library: 80, 187 (*right*); Royal Holloway College, Egham, Surrey (photo A. C. Cooper Ltd): 205; Staatsbibliothek Berlin: 43, 45; Wellcome Historical Medical Museum: 95; Wilkinson-Latham Collection: 237 (*bottom*).

The map on page 98 was designed by Manuel Lopez Parras.

Picture research by Pat Hodgson.

CONTENTS

6 *Acknowledgments*

8 Bird in a Cage

36 Apprenticeship in Harley Street

60 Chaos at Scutari

90 Calamity Unparalleled

118 A Twelvemonth of Dirt

148 The Health of the Army

180 The Nightingale Nurses

212 Governess of India

248 *Bibliography*

250 *Index*

Bird in a Cage

CHAPTER ONE

BIRD IN A CAGE

'I HAD THREE PATHS AMONG WHICH TO CHOOSE. I might have been a literary woman, or a married woman, or a hospital Sister.' When she wrote these words in 1850, Florence Nightingale had rejected the first two paths and, after bitter struggles, virtually given up all hope of the third. 'My God, what will become of me?' she wrote on the last day of that year. 'I have no desire but to die. There is not a night that I do not lie down on my bed, wishing that I may leave it no more. Unconsciousness is all I desire.'

Before the age of thirty, she had gone down into the depths of anguish, defeat and despair. Yet in the material sense she had everything that any young English girl could desire. Well-born, intelligent, good-looking, accomplished, sought-after by eligible young men, admired by a wide circle of friends and relatives, she was lapped round by the love and devotion of her own family. What, then, did she lack? It can be told in one word – freedom. Freedom to pursue the end on which her heart was set, and which she knew to be her true vocation: nursing the sick. In her day, the daughters of the rich and well-born did not nurse the sick. This was a task that, insofar as it was done at all, was left to drunks and whores. Florence Nightingale had pitted herself against the dictates of society and hitherto society had won.

In 1820 the tide of Continental travel by wealthier Britons, released by the end of the Napoleonic wars, was in full flood. Carriages with liveried

PREVIOUS PAGES Embley House, the Nightingales' country home in Hampshire. The house was set in beautifully cultivated parkland, with flower gardens. One of Parthenope's sketches.

postilions were bowling across the Continent; villas and *palazzi* were being rented in Rome, in Venice, in Nice, in Milan; introductions were being presented to Austrian noblemen, Italian revolutionaries, French *savants*, German princelings; paintings, churches, frescoes, ruins and antiquities were all the rage; all was gaiety, conversation and gossip in sunny lands. The young Nightingales were following the fashion when, soon after their marriage in 1818, they set out, with an entourage of servants, for Italy, where they remained for nearly three years. On 12 May 1820 their second daughter was born at the Villa Colombaia, near the Porto Romano in Florence. And it was the city of Florence after which she was named. Her father, William Edward Nightingale, was twenty-five and her mother, Fanny, thirty-two.

Villa Colombaia in Florence, where the Nightingales' second daughter was born. Florence was christened in its drawing-room.

WEN, Florence's father. By nature retiring and studious, he had fallen for his opposite in the vivacious Fanny Smith. In later years he was to withdraw from the bitter quarrels among the women in his family.

Florence's mother, Fanny
Smith. Attractive and lively,
she concentrated on the
social side of life and
cherished strong ambitions
for her daughters.

Her father had been born a Shore of Tapton, in Derbyshire, but changed his name when he came of age and inherited the property of an uncle. When he went up to Cambridge he had an income of between £7,000 and £8,000 a year. He was very tall and thin, studious by nature, contemplative, in outlook liberal, but with a streak of indolence that throughout his life prevented his talents taking shape in any notable achievement, and his will from governing family affairs.

Fanny was a much stronger character. Her grandfather, Samuel Smith, had made a fortune in the City and given generous support to humanitarian causes. His son William followed this tradition, championing Abolitionists, Jews, sweatshop workers and the downtrodden generally, and was for many years a Member of Parliament. He raised ten children, nearly all of whom lived to a ripe old age. The William Smiths were a close-knit, energetic, high-spirited and fertile family, and Florence Nightingale and her elder sister Parthenope grew up amid a tribe of aunts, uncles and first cousins, in whose mansions busy house-parties were continually gathering. Two sets of cousins featured particularly in their lives: the Bonham Carters of Fairoaks near Winchester, and the Nicholsons of Waverley Abbey near Farnham in Surrey.

When Florence was a year old, her parents returned from Italy to settle on their property at Lea Hurst in Derbyshire. A new house had first to be built and Mr Nightingale designed it. It had a magnificent view across the River Derwent and heather-clad hills beyond. 'One seems on a pinnacle,' wrote Mrs Gaskell, 'with the clouds careering round one,' and she commented on the simplicity of what had been the children's nursery: 'the old carpet doesn't cover the floor. No easy chair, no sofa, a little curtainless bed.' Florence grew up to love Lea Hurst and years later, when on the shores of the Bosporus, she wrote: 'How I like to hear that ceaseless roar; it puts me in mind of the dear Derwent; how often have I listened to it from the nursery window.'

But the Nightingales soon decided that Lea Hurst was too cold, too remote and too small – although it had fifteen bedrooms – to become their main residence. In 1825 they bought a property on the edge of the New Forest, Embley Park, in the parish of Wellow near Romsey. Apart from its other advantages, Embley was within easy reach of the Nicholsons and the Bonham Carters. Thereafter the Nightingales spent most of the year at Embley, a spell in London during the 'Season' and the summer months at Lea Hurst.

At first the education of the two girls was entrusted to governesses, but when Florence was twelve, her father took it over. He proved a lively if exacting teacher. A passion for accuracy was one of his legacies to his younger daughter. With him they read Tasso, Ariosto, Alfieri; 'he was a good and always interested Italian scholar,' Florence wrote, 'never pedantic, never a tiresome grammarian, but he spoke Italian like an Italian and I took care of the verbs.' Latin, Greek and French were part of the curriculum; also history, composition and mathematics. Both sisters received a wider, deeper education than most girls of their day. Florence was the better scholar of the two, as well as being the livelier and more attractive girl.

Yet she was often unhappy. For one thing, her relationship with 'Parthe' was uneasy. The sisters loved each other, but not as much as Florence knew they should. 'Pray dear Pop,' she wrote at the age of ten, 'let us love each other better than we have done. It is the will of God and Mamma particularly desires it.' Parthe was jealous of her younger sister's better looks, livelier wit, superiority in lessons. From Fanny's point of view, Parthe was a much more 'normal' daughter, who enjoyed helping her mother with the household tasks and chatting to neighbours. Florence had first place in their father's heart. Even so, he sometimes grew impatient. 'Ask Flo if she has lost her intellect,' he wrote to his wife. 'If not, why does she grumble at troubles which she cannot remedy by grumbling?' She could be difficult, withdrawn, apt to retreat into a world of her own.

All through her youth and early womanhood, she was greatly troubled by a habit of escaping into a fantasy world, which she called 'dreaming'. It was more than just the day-dreaming of a child, though no doubt it grew out of this. She was uncertain of herself, and 'always in mortal fear of doing something unlike other people. . . . I had a morbid terror of not using my knives and forks like other people when I should come out. I was afraid of speaking to children because I was sure I should not please them.' All Florence's feelings were deep and intense to the point where they could become self-destructive. Even when she was in her teens, the bustling round of family visits, the domestic events of that enormous clan – a wedding, an engagement, a christening, a birthday – the constant flow of guests and letters; all this, which so satisfied her mother and sister, began to seem futile and wasteful. She craved for 'some regular occupation, for something worth doing instead of frittering time away on useless trifles'.

When she was not yet seventeen, she received a direct call from God. On 7 February 1837, 'God spoke and called me to His service,' she wrote at Embley. (Throughout her life she was a copious writer of notes, often jotted down on odd scraps of paper, sometimes in the form of a diary.) Biographers have compared this summons with the voice heard by Joan of Arc. One difference seems to have been that God did not say what form that service had to take. It was to be sixteen years – long, weary, continually frustrated years – before she found out.

Meanwhile there were diversions, notably foreign travel. When she was seventeen, in September 1837, the whole family, with six attendants, set forth to revisit Italy, travelling in a leisurely fashion through

A view across the hills of Florence, which the Nightingales revisited in 1837. Travel was one activity which stimulated Florence's interest and relieved the monotony of the social round in London and at Embley.

France in a large coach designed by Mr Nightingale and drawn by three pairs of horses with mounted postilions. Her diary reveals an unusual combination of enthralled response to visual beauty – Chartres Cathedral by moonlight kept her at her window all night – with an intellectual search for facts. Even at this age, she collected statistics: a table exactly recorded distances and times of departure and arrivals, and she kept notes on the laws, land tenure systems and social conditions of the regions through which they passed. She enjoyed herself too. By now knives and forks held no more terrors. Grand balls given by Grand Dukes; a magnificent suite of rooms overlooking the Arno; the glories of the opera in Florence, of which she kept meticulous notes; the excitement of the company of Italian patriots scheming to free their country from Austrian rule – these were indeed a change from the domestic dramas of her Hampshire cousins.

By way of Geneva, aboil with political refugees and sheltering the future Emperor Louis Napoleon, the Nightingales reached Paris in September 1838 and took apartments in the Place Vendôme. That winter Florence made one of the deepest and most lasting friendships of her life. In the Rue du Bac lived, with her daughter Mary, an elderly Mrs Clarke. Doctors had ordered her, after several attacks of bronchitis, to remain indoors for life; whether because of or in spite of obedience to these orders, she lived to be ninety-two. In almost every way her daughter Mary was unusual. She was small, slight, droll, in appearance childlike, with large blue eyes and a mop of hair likened by Guizot to a Yorkshire terrier: in manner vivacious, intelligent, uninhibited, gay. Entirely through her own qualities, she had placed herself in the centre of the most exclusive and critical circle of the Parisian intellectual elite, the world of the *salon*. Madame Récamier had befriended her, and she was the darling of Chateaubriand. Her associates were scholars, men of letters, wits and *savants*. The Clarkes must have kept a good table; Mary believed that 'eating is a pleasure which is beyond all comparison the greatest.' Almost all her friends were men and she had absolutely no time for women. 'Why don't they talk about interesting things? Why don't they use their brains? My dear, they have no manners. I can't abide them in my drawing-room. With their shyness and their inability

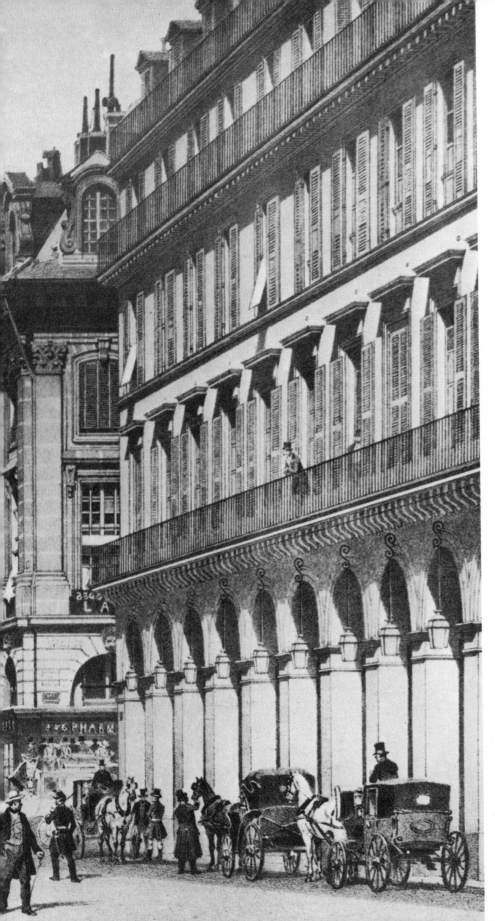

Paris: the fashionable Place Vendôme and rue Castiglione, with the Colonne de la Grande Armée. Here the Nightingales stayed in the autumn of 1838 and here Florence met Mary Clarke for the first time. A mid-nineteenth-century lithograph.

to hold their tongues, they ain't fit for decent company.'

The Nightingales had an introduction to Mary Clarke and were invited to a 'children's soirée'. They found Mary's room full of romping boys and girls. The Nightingale sisters immediately joined in and romped with the best of them. This impressed 'Clarkey', as they came to call her, so favourably that the whole family was invited to one of her Friday evenings, and launched forthwith into Parisian intellectual society. They were presented to Madame Récamier and even invited to hear Chateaubriand read his *Memoires d'Outre-Tombe* at the Abbaye-au-Bois – 'a favour eagerly sought for by the cream of the cream of Paris society at that time', Parthe wrote.

In this congenial atmosphere Florence held her own. If not beautiful, she was elegant and distinguished, and both widely and deeply read. Her shyness had been overcome. She expressed herself pithily, often with a somewhat caustic wit, in perfect French. Under 'Clarkey's' wing they went to parties, balls, museums, operas, concerts, artists' studios. Everyone was happy, not least Fanny who could now feel satisfied that her younger daughter's rebellious moods and fits of moping were but adolescent symptoms; Florence could be gay, entertaining, well-dressed and much admired by men. A good marriage seemed assured.

In April 1839 the family returned to England to resume a busy life divided between Embley, London and Lea Hurst, with visits to Waverley, Fairoaks and other country houses thrown in. Then came the London Season, and both daughters were presented at Court. 'We are enjoying ourselves much,' Florence wrote to Mary Clarke, now a regular correspondent. 'The Nicholsons, our cousins, came up to town the day after we did, and are living in the same hotel. . . . As Marianne Nicholson is as music-mad as I am, we are revelling in music all day long'; and London was 'a perfect whirlwind of excitement for the few days that the Melbourne ministry was out'. In September 1839 they travelled back by rail from Lea Hurst – 'how much pleasanter it is travelling by these public conveyances than in one's own stupid carriage' – with a royal equerry, who told them that 'Lord Melbourne called the Queen's favourite terrier a frightful little beast, and often contradicted her flat, all of which she takes in good part, and lets him go to sleep after dinner, taking care that he shall not be waked.'

Two of her first cousins became Florence's bosom friends. One was Hilary Bonham Carter; the other, Marianne Nicholson – beautiful, audacious, witty, with a true gift for music – bewitched her. 'I never loved but one person with passion in my life and that was her,' Florence wrote several years later. Marianne did not give her heart to Florence but her brother Henry did, and Florence may well have encouraged him in order to bring her closer to Marianne. Poor Henry had to wait six years for his answer. Her refusal opened a breach between the two families and plunged the introspective Florence into an emotional abyss. 'I was not a worthy friend to her [Marianne]. I was not true either to her or to myself in our friendship. I was afraid of her: that is the truth.' The story ended tragically six years later with news from Spain of Henry's death by drowning. In the same year Marianne married Captain Douglas Galton of the Royal Engineers.

It was not long before the futility of the social round, varied now and then by nursing sick relatives, began once more to fret Florence's nerves and oppress her spirit. She was bored: not for lack of employment but because she had employment of the wrong kind. God, having called her to His service, had not spoken again, and for this there could be but one reason: her own unworthiness. This began to prey on her mind.

Today, how simple would her case be. She would amass A-levels, go to a university and emerge with an honours degree – probably in mathematics, for that she thought to be her bent when she launched a rather pathetic effort to find something to bite into and train her mind. She enlisted an ally in her father's sister Mai, an aunt twice over, having married Fanny's brother Sam. Their son Shore, who was to inherit the Nightingale property, became Florence's darling, as she became her aunt Mai's. The mathematics project won Mai Smith's support and she tried to persuade Fanny to agree to the employment of a 'clean middle-aged respectable person' as a teacher. 'I think if she [Florence] had a subject which required *all* her powers and which she pursued regularly and vigorously for a couple of hours, she would be happier all day for it.' To encourage her niece, they had both been getting up at six o'clock –

A portrait of Florence by
Augustus Leopold Egg.
Although she was attractive
to men and attracted by
them, she felt instinctively
that fulfilment in life
demanded a deeper
challenge, which found its
answer at Scutari.

this was in winter, when Florence was paying a family visit – to light a fire and 'sit very comfortably at our work'. It was no use. Mathematics, in Fanny's view, were no subject of study for a marriageable girl; she had much better improve her playing of quadrilles. Aunt Mai persisted, found a teacher who was a married clergyman and promised a chaperon, and one of Fanny's brothers agreed to let them use his library. All that could be achieved was a lesson twice a week for one month, while Florence stayed with her uncle Octavius Smith and looked after his children. Then back to Embley and the social round.

This was not, perhaps, quite as drab as Florence found it. The Nightingales were neighbours of the Palmerstons and became close friends. They got to know the future Lord Shaftesbury, famous for reforms which were after Florence's heart. At the Nicholsons' there was a huge house-party at Christmas 1841, with a grand masked ball and a performance of *The Merchant of Venice* for which Florence was stage-manager. She had difficulties, according to Parthe, with 'a Captain Elliott, fresh from China, who could by no means be brought to obey', and with her uncle Adams Smith who forgot his lines 'tho' Flo had been putting it into him with a sledge-hammer all the week'.

Other entertainments were more sober. At a dinner-party given by her father, Florence sat between an eminent geologist and an Egyptologist no less renowned. The geologist she 'charmed by the breadth of her views, which were not common then', but when she 'proceeded into the realms of Latin and Greek, our geologist had to get out of it'. The Egyptologist did well enough until 'she began quoting Lepsius, which she had been studying in the original, and he was in the same case as Sir Henry'. This story, written down years later by Lady Caroline Fox, indicates that Florence held her own in intellectual as well as in social circles. In London the Nightingales were taken up by the Chevalier de Bunsen (Baron Bunsen after 1857), the Prussian Ambassador, and his rich English wife. He was an Egyptologist of international repute – a friend of Lepsius, which no doubt accounted for Florence's interest in the latter's work – and a supporter of all liberal causes.

Florence much preferred London to the New Forest. It was, she wrote, 'my place of rest. There at least you can have your mornings to yourself.

To me the country is the place of "row".' There were always guests, she was 'forever expected to be looking merry and saying something lively'. But Lea Hurst she loved, with its grandeur, its wildness and the village nearby where she could help and get to know the villagers. Sometimes, according to Mrs Gaskell, she would be missing from the dinner-table and traced to the bedside of a sick person. For here she found the vocation to which God had called her: nursing the sick and needy. This was to be her work in the world. But between resolution and performance arose the enormous, the seemingly impassable barrier of her family's opposition, united with society's rules. Fanny was adamant. She was not a cruel woman, she was fond of her daughter, but when Flo challenged the convictions of her age and sex and class, she could be stubborn as a mule and utterly blind to the passions and yearnings that were eating the heart out of her younger daughter.

One result was that Florence's habit of escaping into 'dreaming' intensified. She would go off into a kind of trance, even in the middle of a dinner-party. She grew alarmed. Surely this was a symptom of mental illness? She was also ashamed, and confided in no one her enslavement to what she regarded as a secret vice. Possibly it saved, rather than threatened, her sanity by offering a safety-valve. She did not see it like this, but as one more proof that God had found her unworthy.

Shuttled continually about between Embley, Lea Hurst, London and various family homes, she also found the lack of continuity distracting. To a Nicholson aunt by marriage, aunt Hannah, she wrote: 'Ask me to do something for your sake, something difficult, and you will see that I shall do it *regularly*, which for me is the most difficult thing of all.' She longed for a routine, a scheme of living to give shape to her life. Instead, it was filled with irritating trivialities. Her father developed the habit of reading *The Times* aloud to his daughters, adding his own as well as editorial comments. 'Now for Parthe, the morning's reading did not matter; she went on with her drawing; but for me, who had no such cover, the thing was boring to desperation.' Reading aloud she thought 'the most miserable exercise of the human intellect. It is like lying on one's back, with one's hands tied, and having liquid poured down one's throat.' She did not think much better of writing. 'You ask me

OPPOSITE *Mrs Nightingale and her Daughters*, a painting by A. E. Chalon which now hangs in Claydon House, the home of the Verneys.

24

why I do not write something,' she wrote to Mary Clarke. 'I had so much rather live than write – writing is only a substitute for living. . . . I think one's feelings waste themselves in words, they ought to be distilled into actions and into actions which bring results.'

Meanwhile she had another suitor, and one to whom she felt much more powerfully drawn than she had to Henry Nicholson. In the summer of 1842, at a dinner-party given by the Palmerstons, she met Richard Monckton Milnes, a young man – he was then thirty-three – described by his biographer as 'one of the ornaments of English society'. He was rich, intelligent, amusing, talented, an extrovert with a remarkable gift for friendship. 'A most bland-smiling, semi-quizzical, affectionate, high-bred, Italianized little man' was Carlyle's description, with 'long live-blonde hair, a dimple, next to no chin'. He 'never forgot an old friend', one of them wrote. 'His wit had no sting in it. He had a great relish for amusement, and a benevolent desire to amuse others.' One of his ways of doing this was to give breakfast parties at his rooms in Pall Mall. These became famous. Milnes's circle included such men as Carlyle, Tennyson, Arthur Hallam, Landor, Baron Bunsen, Thackeray, Guizot, de Tocqueville, and the poets Campbell and Moore. He was a poet himself of polish and sensitivity, but his poetry did not live.

Carlyle remarked that if Christ came again, Richard Monckton Milnes would ask Him to breakfast. Yet Milnes had a serious as well as a social side. He was a first-class linguist, widely travelled and a member of Parliament who in 1846 introduced a Bill to provide reformatories for juveniles – the precursors of Approved Schools – and became president of the first one to be created. A more suitable match for Florence could scarcely have been imagined. Richard Monckton Milnes fell deeply in love with her, and years later Florence was to describe him as 'the man I adored'.

They loved one another, he was rich and eligible, she clever and good-looking, they shared common interests – why did they not marry? Because of Florence's conviction that God had called her to higher things. The year in which she met Richard Monckton Milnes, 1842, was also the year she met de Bunsen, and it was the Chevalier who told her about an institution in Germany which fired her imagination and helped

OPPOSITE A watercolour of Florence, seated and stitching embroidery, with Parthenope. It was painted by W. White in about 1836 when Florence was sixteen.

Richard Monckton Milnes, one of Florence's suitors. They remained friends for life, and Milnes was one of the leading lights behind the launching of the Nightingale Fund in 1855. This chalk drawing is by George Richmond.

to mould her life. This was the Institution of Deaconesses at Kaiserswerth on the Rhine. It had been started by Pastor Theodor Fliedner on a very small scale as an orphanage which expanded to include a school, hospital and penitentiary, and it was the only place that Florence knew of which provided any form of training for women in such work. She had by now realized, as few did in those days, that nursing was not just a matter of kind words, fervent prayers and a little nourishing soup. Nursing was also a technique to be learned like any other. 'I saw a poor woman die before my eyes this summer,' she wrote to her cousin Hilary, 'because there was nothing but fools to sit up with her, who poisoned her as much as if they had given her arsenic.'

In 1846 de Bunsen loaned her an annual report from Kaiserswerth which strengthened her resolve to get herself accepted for such training as it offered – haphazard and incomplete, but at least practical. And at least respectable; her family could not dismiss the Deaconesses as immoral. Even so, it was to be six years before she could, and then only partially, achieve her aim.

During the summer of 1844 the American philanthropist Dr Samuel Gridley Howe came to stay at Embley, and Florence asked him whether he thought it would be 'a dreadful thing' if she were to devote her life to nursing. 'Not a dreadful thing at all,' he replied. 'I think it would be a very good thing.' It would be unusual, and in England anything unusual was regarded as unsuitable, but he encouraged her to 'go forward . . . act up to your inspiration and you will find there is never anything unbecoming or unladylike in doing your duty for the good of others'. Thus fortified, she formed a plan. She would go to Salisbury Infirmary for a few months 'to learn the "prax"'; then come back to nurse at West Wellow and ultimately, she wrote to Hilary: 'I do not much like talking about it, but I thought something like a Protestant Sisterhood, without vows, for women of educated feelings, might be established.'

Of all the efforts Florence made to wriggle off the hook of English mid-nineteenth-century upper-class convention and morality, none aroused more horror and dismay among her family than this idea of going to Salisbury Infirmary to learn the 'prax'. Their fears were not unfounded. Fanny was terrified, her daughter wrote, not only by 'the physically revolting parts of a hospital, but things about surgeons and nurses which you may guess'. Physically revolting, indeed, the hospitals were, in those days before Pasteur's discoveries of how germs spread infection, and Lister's of the use of antiseptics. The huge wards, with beds jam-packed together, were filthy, their floors and walls saturated with blood and ordure, and the 'hospital smell' was such as to induce nausea in anyone entering a ward for the first time. The patients were filthy and verminous; bedding stank and was seldom changed; infections of every kind were prevalent; gangrene was rife. The surgeons with their blood-bespattered clothes and unsterilized knives spread infection as well as agony and terror among their patients. Sometimes their coats, stiff with dried blood, stood up of their own accord when their wearers shed them.

There was no privacy, virtually no sanitation and men and women suffered, protested and died among their fellows in stench, pain, dirt and degradation, relieved, if they were lucky, by gin and brandy smuggled into the wards. Almost all the nurses were women of loose morals and most of them drank. Florence later recalled that 'It was *preferred* that the nurses should be women who had lost their characters, i.e. should have had one child.' They slept in the wards with their patients, sometimes in the less afflicted male patients' beds, otherwise 'in wooden cages on the landing places outside the doors of the wards, where it was impossible for any woman of character to sleep, where it was impossible for the Night Nurse taking her rest during the day to sleep at all owing to the noise, where there was not light or air'. As for 'the things about surgeons and nurses' – sex with the nurses on demand was considered to be a surgeon's perk. To allow Florence to go down into this inferno was unthinkable.

It was an unrealistic idea, but she suffered deeply when it was decisively rejected. 'You will laugh, dear, at the whole plan, I daresay,' she wrote to Hilary Bonham Carter in December 1845, 'but no one but the mother of it knows how precious an infant idea becomes, nor how the soul dies between the destruction of one and the taking up of another. I shall never do anything, and am worse than dust and nothing. . . . Oh for some strong thing to sweep this loathesome life into the past.' In private, she

A cartoon of the 1840s
illustrating the popular idea
of the nurse of the day, a
slattern more interested in
the bottle than in her
patients.

Two more cartoons of nursing before the reforms of Florence Nightingale: RIGHT A typical monthly nurse of the period. OPPOSITE A later cartoon (1879) of the drunken nurse dozing at the bedside of an alarmed patient.

The Nurse — Old Style

gave way to despair and wrote in one of her many scribbled notes: 'I cannot live – forgive me, oh Lord, and let me die, this day let me die.' And again: 'The day of personal hopes and fears is over for me. Now I dread and desire no more.' 'The plough goes over the soul.'

For six years, from the end of 1846 until some time in 1851, Florence lived largely in a hell of her own making. It would not be fair to say that this was simply because she could not get her own way. She believed that God was punishing her for her unworthiness to do His work. 'No one has had such advantages, and I have sinned with all these. . . . No one has so grieved the Holy Spirit,' she wrote. And: 'All that I do is poisoned by the fear that I am not doing it in simplicity and godly sincerity.' The vice of dreaming grew worse. The social round seemed more and more pointless, and the effort of subduing her feelings and acting as a dutiful daughter sickened her quite literally; she had attacks of migraine, bronchitis and chronic coughs, and feared that she was going out of her mind.

Only at Lea Hurst did the clouds lift. 'O happy, happy six weeks at the Hurst,' she wrote after she had been nursing sick villagers. 'I found my business in this world. My heart was filled. My soul was at home. I wanted no other heaven.' But she was snatched back to London and Hampshire, and her health grew worse again. By the autumn of 1847 she was clearly on the verge of a nervous breakdown.

She was rescued by Charles and Selina Bracebridge, a middle-aged childless couple who proved to be among her dearest and most faithful and unselfish friends. They took her to Rome, and there, among new sights and scenes and in congenial and affectionate company, her spirits quickly revived. 'I never enjoyed any time in my life as much as my time in Rome.' Antiquities, churches, the catacombs, all enthralled her, and there was plenty of activity: sight-seeing, riding in the Campagna, plant collecting; above all her religious sense was transported by the works of Michelangelo. She spent a whole day in the Sistine Chapel alone with Selina 'looking up into that heaven of angels and prophets', and the impression stamped on her mind was never erased; prints of the Sistine frescoes were hanging in the room where she died. In Rome she enjoyed 'the most entire and unbroken freedom from dreaming that I ever had'.

It was in Rome, early in 1848, that the most important encounter in her life took place. Through the Bracebridges, she met Sidney Herbert. The former Secretary at War in Sir Robert Peel's government was wintering in Italy with the bride he had married about a year before, Elizabeth à Court. The five English travellers soon became bosom companions and friends.

Sidney Herbert was a half-brother of the Earl of Pembroke, and heir to the famous Wilton House in Wiltshire. He had everything: good looks – a face not only handsome but sweet in its expression; great intelligence; wit allied to a genuine love of his fellow-men; modesty, charm, grace of manner; he was moreover an excellent shot and a bold rider to hounds. He was a devout Christian. He was exceedingly rich. His Parliamentary career, at that moment interrupted by the fall of Peel's ministry, had begun with promise, and was sure to be resumed with success. Many good causes drew on his support, and charity began at home with the well-treated tenants of his estate. He and Florence clearly had everything in common. Herbert's wife, known as Liz, was almost equally attractive and became Florence's close friend. There was no scandal, nor cause for one. Yet if Sidney Herbert had not fallen under Florence's spell in Rome, there would have been no Lady with a Lamp at Scutari.

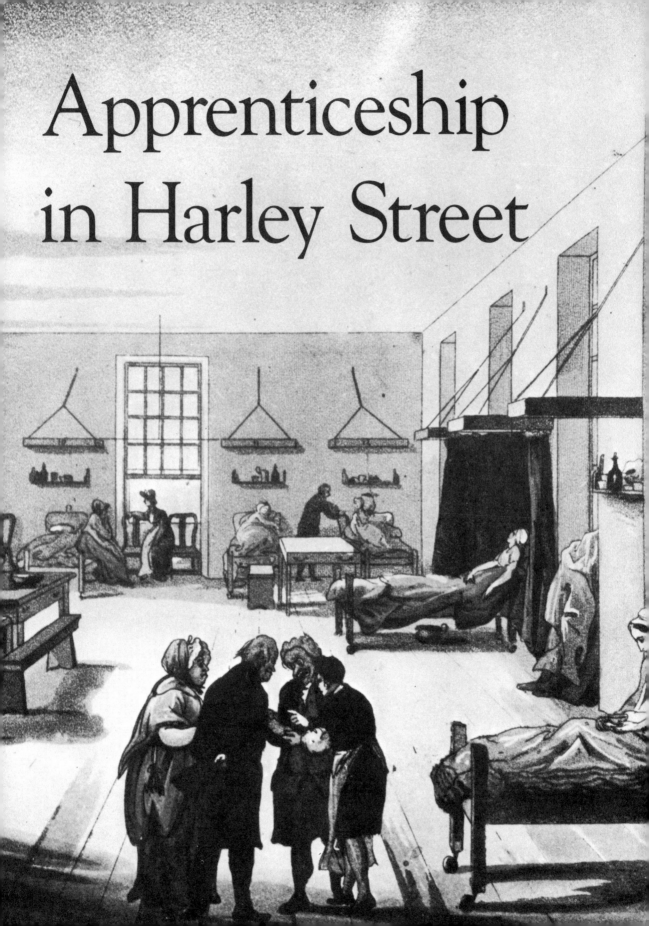

Apprenticeship
in Harley Street

♔ CHAPTER TWO

APPRENTICESHIP IN
HARLEY STREET

WHEN FLORENCE REJOINED HER FAMILY at home, nothing had changed. The dreary round of social life started up again. Aunt Hannah, to whom she complained, assured her that even a dinner-party could redound to the glory of God. 'How can it be to the glory of God,' she retorted, 'when there is so much misery among the poor, which we might be curing instead of living in luxury?' To give her an occupation, Fanny set her to check long lists of household plate, linen, kitchen equipment and stores. 'Can reasonable people want all this?' she asked herself – while the poor lived in such destitution.

Her fantasies came back in full force; they were the reality, English country life the dream.

In an English country place everything that is painful is so carefully removed out of sight, behind those fine trees, to a village three miles off. In London, at all events if you open your eyes, you cannot help seeing in the next street that life is not as it has been made to you. You cannot get out of a carriage at a party without seeing what is in the faces making the lane on either side, and without feeling tempted to rush back and say, 'Those are my brothers and sisters.'

PREVIOUS PAGES The caricaturist Thomas Rowlandson's impression of a ward inside the Middlesex Hospital in 1808. Once again plenty of alcohol is in evidence.

Despite the Salisbury calamity, Florence's interest in hospitals intensified. If she could not work in one, at least she could learn all about them – how they were organized, the improvements that were needed and here and there being made, such statistics as were kept about causes of mortality, and so on. In 1847 Mary Clarke had, at the age of fifty-four,

Florence in 1854. This was the year in which the great opportunity of her lifetime came, when she set off for Scutari to take charge of the nursing of soldiers wounded in the Crimea. This revelation of God's purpose for her life put an end to the 'dreaming' which had hitherto afflicted her.

married a man seven years her junior, Julius Mohl. An Oriental scholar of distinction, born a German, he had taken French nationality in order to be near the remarkable woman he eventually married. He was a charming, cultivated and kind-hearted man, who shared Mary's affec- tion for Florence and did much to help her. The Mohls in Paris and the de Bunsens in London gathered for her reports from all over Europe about matters relating to the care of the sick. These she analysed, collated and digested with such diligence that she came to know more about hospitals and hospital reform than almost anyone living.

Nor had she relinquished hope of studying at Kaiserswerth. She enlisted influential friends such as Lord Ashley and the de Bunsens to talk her parents over.

In September 1848 Fanny reluctantly agreed to let her visit Kaisers- werth for a few weeks while the rest of the family stayed with the Mohls at Frankfurt. Then, in this revolutionary year, came news of disturbances and dangers, the whole plan fell through and the Nightingales went to Malvern instead. Florence was thrown back into the depths of despair.

She cannot have been a cheerful companion at this period, yet the gay, convivial and generous-hearted Richard Monckton Milnes had not abandoned his suit. Florence continued to prevaricate, neither dismissing nor encouraging him. He waited seven years for an answer. At last, in the summer of 1849, he would wait no longer. The answer was 'no'.

It was an extraordinarily brave decision. With her youth all but over, she was most unlikely to have another chance. Milnes sympathized with her hopes and loved her. All doors to the life she longed to lead seemed to be barred and bolted. She was living in the black despair of those who believed themselves abandoned by their God. As the wife of one of the élite among Britain's rulers, and one who shared her reforming zeal, many opportunities to advance her aims would surely come her way. She would be freed from the tyranny of her family, freed probably from her curse of 'dreaming' and free to work towards the causes she believed in. Yet she turned him down.

I have an intellectual nature which requires satisfaction, and that would find it in him. I have a passional nature which requires satisfaction, and that would find it in him. I have a moral, an active nature which requires satisfaction, and that would not find it in his life. I can hardly find satisfaction for any of my natures. . . . I could be satisfied to spend a life with him combining our different powers in some great object. I could not satisfy this nature by spending a life with him in making society and arranging domestic things. . . . To be nailed to a continuation and exaggeration of my present life, without hope of another, would be intolerable to me. Voluntarily to put it out of my power ever to be able to seize the chance of forming for myself a true and rich life would seem to me like suicide.

And so Richard Monckton Milnes went out of her life. Her family was furious. The tensions grew. She paid a heavy price for her decision. 'Since I refused him, not one day has passed without my thinking of him, life is desolate without his sympathy.' The nervous breakdown that had threatened for several years was now so imminent that the Bracebridges once again came to the rescue and persuaded Fanny to let them take her to Egypt.

They set off in November 1849, and early in January 1850 ascended the first Cataract, to Florence 'one of the most delightful moments of my life'. The temple of Ipsamboul, their most southerly point, was 'the only thing that has ever made an impression on me like that of St Peter's'. On the way back down the Nile, at Karnak in March 1850, as she sat on the steps of the portico, God spoke to her again and 'asked me would I do good for Him alone without the reputation'. Two days later, alone in her cabin, she 'settled the question with God', and for about a fortnight was 'undisturbed by my great enemy' (her dreaming). It was a temporary respite. In April they moved on to Athens where she wrote 'I have felt here the suspension of all my faculties, I could not write, could not read. . . .' And on her birthday, 12 May, there came the heartbroken note: 'Today I am thirty – the age Christ began his mission. Now no more childish things. No more love. No more marriage. Now Lord let me think only of Thy Will, what thou willest me to do. Oh Lord, Thy Will, Thy Will.'

She was too ill to enjoy the sights of Athens, but there was one bright spot when she bought a baby owl that had just fallen out of its nest in the Parthenon, and, after calming it by mesmerism, carried it about in her

Athena, Florence's pet owl:
a pen-and-wash drawing
from Claydon House.

pocket. She named it Athena. In June 1850, 'after a sleepless night
physically and morally ill and broken down, a slave – glad to leave
Athens. I had no wish on earth but to sleep.' And the next day: 'My
enemy is too strong for me, everything has been tried. . . . All is in vain.'
She felt she was 'rapidly approaching the state of madness when dreams
become realities'. On 1 July she 'lay in bed and called on God to save me'.

It was an inspiration of the Bracebridges to take her to Berlin, where
instead of ruins there were hospitals and orphanages to see. Her spirits
revived. And then, at long last, Kaiserswerth. 'With the feeling with
which a pilgrim first looks on the Kedron, I saw the Rhine, dearer to
me than the Nile.' They stayed only a fortnight, but it gave her a 'feeling
so brave as if nothing could ever vex me again'. At Ghent, in six days,
she wrote a pamphlet describing the work of the Institution, which was
published anonymously later in the same year.

Fanny was furious about the Kaiserswerth visit and, once back among
her 'dear people', all Florence's euphoria drained away. Parthe had
hysterics, her father as usual refused to take sides, the old routine closed

about her like a cocoon. Once more she was tormented, and her sense of guilt returned. God had withdrawn because of her sins. On the last day of 1850 she wrote: 'My present life is suicide. Slowly, I have opened my eyes to the fact that I cannot now deliver myself from the habit of dreaming which, like gin drinking, is eating out my vital strength. Now I have let myself go entirely.... I have no desire but to die. There is not a night that I do not lie down on my bed, wishing that I may leave it no more.' And a few weeks later: 'Oh, how am I to get through this day, to talk through all this day, is the thought of every morning.... In my thirty-first year I see nothing desirable but death.... Why, oh my God, can I not be satisfied with the life that satisfies so many people? ... My God, what am I to do?'

So much suffering – and the remedy such a simple one. All that was needed was her parents' permission to go back to Kaiserswerth. The Nightingales were a stubborn family. No one would give way.

At last, to save her sanity, Florence decided to take matters into her own hands. With or without her family's approval, she would go back

A woodcut of the Institution of Deaconesses at Kaiserswerth. Pastor Theodor Fliedner and his wife laid the foundations of the Institution when they converted their summer-house to accommodate a discharged prisoner. By 1851 it embraced a hospital, a penitentiary, an orphan asylum, an infant school and a training school for teachers.

43

to Kaiserswerth. In June 1851 she wrote: 'I must expect no sympathy or help from them. I must *take* some things, as few as I can, to enable me to live. I must *take* them, they will not be given to me.' For years she had refused to face this hard fact, and even now she had not abandoned all hope that her 'beloved people', even if they would not help her, would at least come to acquiesce. Parthe was ill and was to take the cure at Carls-bad. Florence delivered her ultimatum. She would leave her family and spend the three months they were to be in Carlsbad at the Institute of Deaconesses. There was no acquiesence, but appalling family rows. At Carlsbad, Parthe had hysterics and threw her bracelets in the face of her sister, who fainted. Florence left next day.

Life at Kaiserswerth was spartan. The trainees were up at 5 a.m., had ten minutes for a slice of bread and a bowl of rye gruel just before 6 a.m., and then worked through till noon when they had a ten-minute break for broth with vegetables. They were allowed another short break at 3 p.m., for tea with bread, and a final bowl of broth at 7 p.m., followed most evenings by a Bible lesson. 'The food was poor,' she afterwards recalled, and as for the nursing, it was 'nil. The hygiene horrible. The hospital was certainly the worst part of Kaiserswerth. I took all the training there was to be had – there was none to be had in England. But Kaiserswerth was far from having trained me.' What it lacked in expertise it made up in the spirit of dedication, service and love: 'Pastor Fliedner's addresses were the very best I ever heard.' There was a lot of praying, mostly informally as the day went on, about anything and everything; and there was also a lot of gaiety. 'For the children there were perpetual birthdays . . . dressing up, with flowers, telling stories, singing, every birthday child asked its own guests and I was always asked. My bad German and foreign stories amused them.' 'The world here fills my life with interest and strengthens me in mind and body,' she wrote home.

Fanny was disturbed by a report that her daughter had been seeing sights unfit for the eyes of gentlewomen. 'The operation to which Mrs Bracebridge alludes', Florence wrote, 'was an amputation at which I was present, but which I did not mention to Parthe, knowing that she would see no more in my interest in it than the pleasure dirty boys have in playing in the puddles about a butcher's shop.' She added: 'This is

Life. Now I know what it is to live and to love life, and really I should be sorry now to leave life. I know you will be glad to hear this, dearest Mum. God has indeed made life rich in interests and blessings, and I wish for no other earth, no other world but this.'

But still her family withheld their blessing. She tried once more to touch her mother's heart. From Kaiserswerth, 31 August 1851, she wrote:

I should be happy here as the day is long, if I could hope that I had your smile, your blessing, your sympathy upon it; without which I cannot be quite happy. My beloved people, I cannot bear to grieve you. Life and everything in it that charms you, you would sacrifice for me; but unknown to you is my thirst, unseen by you are waters which would save me. . . . Oh how shall I show you love and gratitude in return, yet not so perish that you chiefly would mourn. Give me time, give me faith. Trust me, help me. I feel within me that I could gladden your loving hearts which now I wound. . . .

Pastor Theodor Fliedner: a contemporary woodcut. He referred to Florence as 'the Mother of Israel'. She became a close friend, and the godmother of one of the Fliedners' children. When Fliedner died in 1864, she paid for this child's education.

To this emotional, pathetic appeal she received no answer. Fanny tried to keep her daughter's whereabouts a secret from her friends, almost as if Florence had retreated to some hideout to have an abortion. 'They would hardly speak to me,' Florence wrote after her return. 'I was treated as if I had come from committing a crime.' To Mary Mohl, Fanny wrote scathingly: 'Well, I hope Florence will be able to apply all the fine things she has been learning, to do a little to make us better. Parthe and I are much too idle to help and too apt to be satisfied with things as they are.'

Florence was given no chance to apply the fine things she had learned. Soon she was back as hopelessly as ever on the family treadmill. Her father was suffering from inflamed eyes and would undergo treatment at a clinic in Warwickshire only if Florence went with him, submitting to the usual boredom, though she may have been spared the reading aloud. Then came another London Season, more time-wasting than ever. She started a novel, *Cassandra*, which she never finished, and poured into it some of her own frustrations. Women, she wrote, suffered intensely from an accumulation of unused nervous energy which 'makes them feel, every night, when they go to bed as if they were going mad'. But there was one clear gain: she had at last overcome the vice of day-dreaming. On her thirty-second birthday she wrote to her father: 'I hope now that I have come into possession of myself. . . . I hope that I may live, a thing which I have not often been able to say, because I think I have learnt something it would be a pity to waste.'

But waste it she would, if Fanny had her way. Her mother's obstinacy became almost obsessive, and Parthe's jealousy and resentment were such that it was she, not Florence, who had a nervous breakdown. Her sister, of course, had to nurse her out of it. But nothing now could break Florence's resolution. Through Cardinal Manning, she arranged to spend a period at a hospital run by the Sisters of Charity in Paris: Protestant or Catholic, it was all one to her so long as nursing the sick was the end product. Fanny argued, prevaricated, changed her mind, and before her daughter could escape to Paris a great-aunt was taken ill and Florence had to nurse her until she died. 'It has been a baptism of fire this year,' she wrote on the year's last day. But she was no longer despondent. 'All my admirers are married . . . and I stand with all the world before me.' So it proved: 1853 was to be the year of her liberation.

In February 1853 she went with her cousin Hilary to stay with the Mohls in Paris and then to enter for a short period the Maison de la Providence, belonging to the Sœurs de la Charité. At the last moment came the news that her grandmother, aged ninety-five, had been taken ill. Back she had to go to nurse the old lady through her last days. Despite this blow, she was able to write: 'I shall never be thankful enough that I came.' She had done some small things 'which perhaps soothed the awful passage, and which perhaps would not have been done as well without me'.

In April 1853 a movement was afoot to reorganize an Institution for the Care of Sick Gentlewomen in London, run by a charitable committee headed by Lady Canning. A superintendent was needed, and Florence's friend Liz Herbert put forward her name. The committee reacted favourably. Florence was by no means enamoured of charitable ladies and echoed Mary Mohl's description of them as 'fashionable asses'. Negotiations became protracted and involved. To counteract her youth, she was to bring at her own expense an elderly, respectable woman as housekeeper. Although 'no Surgeon Students or Improper Patients' would be there, her family fought the proposal tooth and nail. Threats, hysterics, fainting fits, recriminations so poisoned the air of their rooms in Old Burlington Street that Mr Nightingale retreated to the Athenaeum, where he drafted a despairing note to Parthe: he had 'come to the resolution that it is entirely beyond your mental strength to give up interference in your sister's affairs, and being equally sure that your health cannot stand the strain, we wish to advise you to retire from London and take to your books and country occupations. . . .' Three days later he added 'I doubt my own thoughts.' It was not from her father that Florence inherited her iron resolution and craving for an active, useful life. But Mr Nightingale did take one positive step: despite his wife's anger, he made his daughter an allowance of £500 a year.

The dogs barked furiously; the Fashionable Asses' caravan rumbled slowly on; and when the dust had settled, Florence was installed for the first time in her life in an independent command in the Institution's new premises at Number 1, Harley Street. At the age of thirty-three, on 12

A typical meeting of the
Board of Health at Gwydyr
House, Whitehall: a
drawing from an issue of
The Illustrated London News
in 1849.

August 1853, she was at long last launched on her career.

For the next fourteen months, she had scarcely a moment of leisure. She took over an empty house ten days before the patients were due to move in. In that ten days the alterations had to be completed, furniture installed, everything from pots and pans to carpets and curtains organized. And Florence's ideas were revolutionary. The comfort of the patients and the well-being of the nurses were central to her plan. Unheard-of devices were proposed: bells fitted with 'a valve which flies open when the bell rings, and *remains* open in order that the nurse may see who has rung'; a 'windlass installation' (i.e. a lift) to bring up the patients' meals from the kitchen. All her ideas were intensely practical. She instituted bulk-buying instead of deliveries of 'everything by the ounce', had jam made in the kitchen at a cost of $3\frac{1}{2}$d a pound instead of buying it for a shilling; got bits of spare material from Embley to cover chairs and 'contrived bed covers out of old curtain', brought about 'a complete revolution as to Diet, which is shamefully abused at present', and saved the committee £150 a year by combining the offices of House Surgeon and dispenser.

Her titled committee ladies were at first aghast; instead of a ministering angel, they found they had taken on a human dynamo, and an imperious one at that. There was a sharp brush over the sectarian question. The ladies' committee (there were two committees, one for each sex) wanted only members of the Church of England to be admitted. Florence insisted that any woman who was sick and poor, regardless of her faith, could come. There was a compromise.

So now it is settled, and *in print* that we are to take all denominations what-soever, and allow them to be visited by their respective priests and Muftis, provided *I* will receive (in any case *whatsoever* that is *not* of the Church of England) the obnoxious animal at the door, take him upstairs myself, remain while he is conferring with his patient, make myself *responsible* that he does not speak to, or look at, *anyone else*, and bring him downstairs again in a noose, and out into the street. And to this I have agreed! And this is in print! Amen.

Her main difficulty was to find nurses. There were absolutely none who were properly trained. Nor were the doctors always helpful; when

it came to discharging patients, 'my Committee have not the courage to discharge a single case. The Medical Men say *they* won't, although the cases, they say, *must* be discharged. And I always have to do it, as the stop-gap on all occasions.'

She had described herself well – the stop-gap on all occasions; and these included the actual nursing. As to her talent for this art, there are two opinions. One was her sister's, expressed in a letter to Mary Mohl.

I wish she could be brought to see that it is the intellectual part which interests her, not the manual. She has no *esprit de conduite* in the practical sense. When she nursed me, everything which intellect and kind human intention could do was done but she was a shocking nurse. Whereas her influence on people's minds and her curiosity in getting into varieties of minds is insatiable. After she has got inside, they generally cease to have any interest for her.

The other view was expressed, often in some half-articulate note or broken phrase, by an enormous number of her patients who perhaps expected less, and evidently received more, than her sister. 'Thank you, thank you, darling Miss Nightingale.' 'My dearest kind Miss Nightingale I send you a few lines of love.' 'Were you to give up, all would soon fade away and the whole thing would cease to be.' Such were the notes written by her Harley Street patients. She would go round the wards rubbing their cold feet at night; one patient 'jumped out of bed when FN was coming round and stood with her feet upon the hearth-stone in order to have them rubbed'. The work was incessant but she loved it all and in December 1853 wrote, 'I am now in the heyday of my power.' She had even found out how to manage committees, as she explained to her father. 'When I entered into service here, I determined that, happen what would, I *never* would intrigue among the Committee. Now I perceive that I do all my business by intrigue. I propose in private to A, B or C the resolution I think A, B or C most capable of carrying in committee, and then leave it to them, and I always win.'

In August 1854 an outbreak of cholera swept through the foetid slums of Soho. Florence volunteered to help with the emergency and found herself nursing dying prostitutes and drunken bawds at the Middlesex Hospital, undressing them, 'putting on turpentine stupes',

OPPOSITE Sidney Herbert, the man who did so much to further Florence's work and to whom she was devoted. This portrait by F. Grant was painted in about 1847.

53

Elizabeth Gaskell: a
portrait in chalk by George
Richmond. Mrs Gaskell
was impressed by Florence's
singlemindedness. She was
herself a humanitarian who
in her novels dealt with
subjects, such as the plight
of the unmarried mother,
which were taboo to her
readers.

holding them in her arms as they died. On one occasion she was on her feet without a break for forty-eight hours. 'The prostitutes came in perpetually,' she told Mrs Gaskell in October 1854, 'poor creatures staggering off their beat! It took worse hold of them than of any. One poor girl, loathesomely filthy, came in, and was dead in four hours.'

A touch of humour could be extracted even from such scenes. Mrs Gaskell recorded:

I never heard such capital mimicry as she gave of a poor woman, who was brought in one night, when FN and a porter were the only people up – every other nurse worn out for the time. Three medical students came up, smoking cigars, and went away. FN undressed the woman, who was half tipsy but kept saying, 'You would not think it ma'am, but a week ago I was in silk and satins; in silk and satins dancing at Woolwich. Yes! ma'am, for all I am so dirty I am draped in silks and satins sometimes. Real French silks and satins.' This woman was a nurse earning her five guineas a week with nursing ladies. She got better.

When the epidemic subsided, Florence took a brief holiday at Lea Hurst where Mrs Gaskell, the author of *Cranford*, was a guest. In two

Lea Hurst, the original home of the Nightingales: a sketch by Parthenope. It is now an old people's home.

letters to her friends Emily and Catherine Winkworth, she wrote:

Florence takes up one thing at a time and bends her whole soul to that. Music was it once . . . the scientific part; and for the time cared for nothing but music. Then again the study of the truth as disguised in the myths and hieroglyphics of the Egyptian religion took hold of her, and for a year and a half in Egypt and Athens she was absorbed in this. Now all this is swept away. . . . She never reads any books now. She has not time for it, to begin with; and secondly she says life is so vivid that books seem poor. . . .

FN has very seldom told her family of her plans till they were pretty well matured. . . . I saw a little instance of this when she was here. She had had the toothache, and an abscess in her mouth, and Mrs N was very anxious about her, as she was evidently not strong. On Monday she said, 'I am going to-morrow.' This took them quite by surprise as she evidently was still very poorly; and Mrs N remonstrated.

But Florence went; her family 'had nothing to do but to yield'. Parthe commented: 'She seems led by something higher than I can see, and all I can do is to move every obstacle in my power out of her path.' Mrs Gaskell admired Florence intensely, but found that despite all her compassion for the sick, there was a certain coldness about her.

She has no friend – and she wants none. She stands perfectly alone, half-way between God and His creatures. She used to go a great deal among the villagers here, who dote upon her. . . . She will not go among them now because her heart and soul are absorbed by her hospital plans, and as she says she can only attend to one thing at once. She is so excessively soft and gentle in voice, manner, and movement that one never feels the unbendableness of her character when one is near her. Her powers are astonishing. . . . She is, I think, too much for institutions, sisterhoods and associations. . . . This want of love for individuals becomes a gift and a very rare one, if one takes it in conjunction with her intense love for the *race*; her utter unselfishness in serving and ministering. . . . She is so like a saint.

Unexpectedly, this saint had a gay side to her; the gift for mimicry Mrs Gaskell had mentioned, and 'grey eyes which are generally pensive and drooping, but when they choose can be the merriest eyes I ever saw;

William Howard Russell, The *Times* correspondent whose vivid on-the-spot reports from the Crimea set a new standard in war journalism. This photograph of him in the field was taken by Roger Fenton, whose impressions of the Crimean War are some of the masterpieces of early photography.

THE WAR IN THE CRIMEA.

THE OPERATIONS OF THE SIEGE.

[The following appeared in our second edition of yesterday :—]

(FROM OUR SPECIAL CORRESPONDENT.)

HEIGHTS BEFORE SEBASTOPOL, OCT. 19.

The enemy scarcely fired a shot during the night of the 18th. Our batteries were equally silent. The French, on their side, opened a few guns on their right attack, which they had been working to get into position all night; but they did not succeed in firing many rounds before the great preponderance of the enemy's metal made itself felt, and their works were damaged seriously ; in fact, their lines, though nearer to the enemy's batteries than our own in some instances, were not sufficiently close for the light brass guns with which they were armed. At daybreak the firing continued as usual from both sides. The Russians, having spent the night in repairing the batteries, were nearly in the same position as ourselves, and, unaided or at least unassisted to the full extent we had reason to expect by the French, we were just able to hold our own during the day. Some smart affairs of skirmishers and sharp shooters took place in front. Our riflemen annoy the Russian gunners greatly, and prevent the tirailleurs from showing near our batteries. On one occasion the Russian riflemen and our own men came close upon each other in a quarry before the town. Our men had exhausted all their ammunition ; but as soon as they saw the Russians ...

The Russians have suffered a severe loss in the death of this officer, whose name may be familiar to some readers in connexion with the Sinope expedition.

OCTOBER 20.

Two 68-pounders were mounted last night in our batteries, and the firing, which nearly ceased after dark, was renewed by daybreak. We are all getting tired of this continual "pound-pounding," which makes a great deal of noise, wastes much powder, and does very little damage. It is very hard to batter down earthworks. Most people about London have seen the Artillery butt at Woolwich. How long has it lasted our " heavy fire " of artillery ? Then, again, the Russians have plenty of labourers. They easily repair at night what we destroy and damage during the day. It is difficult for us to do the same. Our men are worn out with fatigue ; the daily service exhausts them, and the artillerymen cannot have more than five hours' rest in the 24. They are relieved every eight hours, but it takes them three hours to get down to their work and return from it to the camp. Our amateurs are quite disappointed and tired out. I fear so are people in England, but they must have patience. Rome was not built in a day, nor will Sebastopol be taken in a week. In fact, we have run away with the notion that it was a kind of pasteboard city, which would tumble down at the sound of our cannon as the walls of Jericho fell at the blast of Joshua's trumpet. The news that Sebastopol had fallen, which we received *viâ* England, has excited great indignation and ludicrous astonishment here. The whole army is enraged about it, as they feel the verity, whatever it may be and whenever it may be realized, must fall short of the effect of that splendid figment. They ...

are still act[...] explosions—[...] Russians'—t[...]

Last nigh[...] mann, and [...] order to siler[...] the Second I[...]

The steam[...] harbour, an[...] our men. S[...] accuracy, ar[...] others befor[...] traverse was[...] hauled off. 2[...] to open in t[...] under Major[...] begun this[...] silent last ni[...]

On the le[...] traverses an[...] battery was[...] a new batte[...] fire on the sl[...] the left and[...] will not be f[...] This is a goo[...] things are ex[...]

Lord Dunb[...] eldest son of[...] prisoner this[...] party of his[...] out of their[...] observed thr[...] in front of t[...] claimed one o[...] fallen " said[...]

An extract from one of William Russell's despatches for *The Times*. Military officials ignored him, and Russell wrote: 'Lord Raglan never spoke to me in his life. . . . I was regarded as a mere camp follower, whom it would be impossible to take more notice of than you would of a crossing sweeper, without the gratuitous penny.'

and perfect teeth, making her smile the sweetest I ever saw. . . . She has a great deal of fun, and is carried along by that, I think.'

All in all, Mrs Gaskell found this young woman very much of an enigma: perhaps 'a creature of another race, so high and mighty and angelic, doing things by impulse or some divine inspiration. . . . She seems too holy to be talked about as a mere wonder.'

At Lea Hurst Mrs Gaskell was companioned by Athena the owl from the Parthenon – 'a regular mischievous intelligent pet'. Athena died a year later, on the eve of Florence's departure for Scutari; on seeing its dead body, she burst into tears.

Already Florence was finding Number 1, Harley Street too limited. Hospital reform was in the air, and the Herberts were closely concerned. The key, as Florence had long known, was the training of competent nurses. King's College Hospital was being rebuilt and, through one of her medical supporters, the suggestion was put forward that she might become its Superintendent of Nurses. In the autumn of 1854 she was busy with plans for recruiting farmers' daughters as probationers and training them on Kaiserswerth lines.

Other things were in store. In March 1854 war had been declared on Russia by England and France. The Russians were besieging the Turks, and in June a British army landed at Varna, on the western shore of the Black Sea, to go to their aid. This help was not called upon, and cholera broke out among the troops. They were embarked in an inadequate number of transports, leaving behind much of their equipment including medical supplies, and taken across the Black Sea to the Crimean penin-sula, with the object of capturing the strongly-fortified Russian naval base at Sebastopol. On 14 September they disembarked at a bay omin-ously called Kalamita, and on the 20th fought the savage battle of the Alma. It was a glorious but a bloody victory, and casualties were high. The aftermath was a revelation of the total inadequacy, indeed almost non-existence, of arrangements to cope with the sick and wounded. Despatches reaching London in mid-October 1854 from the *Times* correspondent, William Howard Russell, shocked the nation; action was called for, and speedy action there was. On 21 October Florence Nightingale set out from London for the Bosporus with a rag-tag and bobtail of thirty-eight hastily assembled women, ranging from Roman Catholic nuns to drunken drabs. The great enterprise for which it seemed, and she believed, fate had in devious ways been gradually and harshly shaping her, was at last in train.

CHAPTER THREE

Chaos at Scutari

CHAOS AT SCUTARI

RUSSELL'S FIRST DESPATCH was published in *The Times* on 9 October 1854. Until its appearance, no one had suspected that all was not well with the forces in the Crimea. Further despatches published on 12 and 13 October revealed a truly appalling state of affairs. Some twenty-seven thousand British troops had crossed the Black Sea from Varna to Kalamita Bay, packed into transports whose wakes were marked by cholera victims flung overboard which, as they decomposed, bobbed to the surface, bloated and horrible. When the troops disembarked, many were too weak to carry their packs, and none had rations beyond three days' supply of salt pork and biscuits. In the four hot September days spent on the shores of the bay awaiting action, over a thousand men, aside from the many who died, were sent back to the transports suffering from cholera.

On 19 September 1854 the united French and British armies, sixty-three thousand strong, advanced to martial music, glittering in their gorgeous uniforms, in brilliant sunshine, across the Crimean plain – 'a sight of inexpressible grandeur', Russell reported. The grandeur was a façade. Long before the first shots were fired, men were falling out in agony from cholera, others suffering torments from thirst. Soon the plain was strewn with discarded equipment, abandoned weapons, dying and exhausted men. That an army in such dire condition should attack a powerful enemy strongly entrenched in a seemingly impregnable position and, against all the odds, defeat them, was a miracle of courage, endurance

PREVIOUS PAGES The disastrous charge of the Light Brigade at Balaclava on 25 October 1854, in which 505 out of 700 cavalrymen lost their lives. Lord Cardigan was generally blamed for his misinterpretation of Raglan's cavalry order. A contemporary artist's impression.

and indomitable morale. Their countrymen had good cause for pride when they read the story of the crossing of the Alma, the storming of the heights above and the retreat into Sebastopol of the powerful Russian army. All the greater was the shock when they learned also of the sufferings to which the sick and wounded survivors had been condemned by official incompetence.

The advance upon Sebastopol was no hasty, unexpected event; it had been discussed for months and was the known objective of the campaign. Plans had, indeed, been made to deal with the wounded. The Turks had handed over to the British their large barracks with its hospital at Scutari, just across the Bosporus from Constantinople. There had been plenty of time to assemble medical supplies and an adequate staff. The cholera outbreak was the first unforeseen challenge. Over a thousand sick men filled the hospital and overflowed into the barracks which the medical staff were told to convert into an emergency hospital. This order, like so many others in the Crimea, was impossible to carry out satisfactorily. The huge building was bare of beds or any furniture, filthy,

The Turkish barracks at Scutari which was made over to the British for use as a hospital. This drawing, showing the cemetery in front of the hospital, is by William Simpson, who made many sketches of the scenes of the Crimean War.

damp and insanitary, and in design entirely unfitting to become a hospital. Even before the first battle casualties arrived, the staff was overwhelmed. Almost everything needed to equip a hospital was lacking, even down to bandages; the orderlies were 'worn-out pensioners' and 'totally useless'; even if a surgeon attended to a man, there were no nurses or dressers to carry out his orders. To rub in the disgrace, the French had plenty of equipment, and Sisters of Charity had 'accompanied the expedition in incredible numbers' (journalistic licence: there were actually fifty).

A storm of indignation followed. *The Times*, under its editor Delane at the peak of its power, opened a fund to succour the sick and wounded. 'Why have we no Sisters of Charity?' *The Times* demanded. But we had. They were not so named, not organized nor in the right place; but they were waiting in the wings. The time had come for them to take the stage.

The British Army was responsible to two masters. There was the Secretary of State *for* War, then the Duke of Newcastle; he doubled the

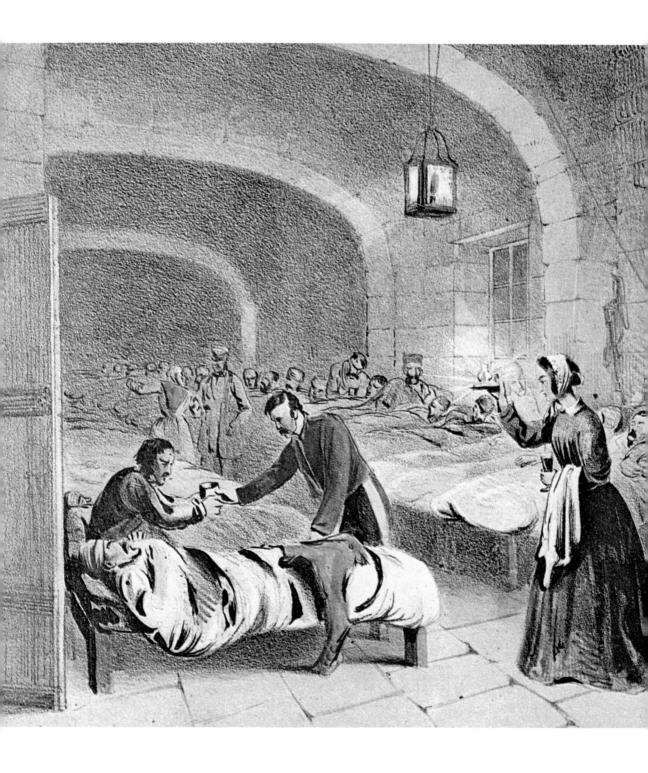

OPPOSITE Benwell's sketch of a ward at the hospital at Scutari. In the centre, Florence holds up her lamp. She transformed the wards beyond recognition.

PREVIOUS PAGES Florence at the entrance to Scutari Hospital: the well-known painting by J. Barrett. Through the archway is a view of the harbour.

LEFT Dr Andrew Smith's new ambulance waggon, used at the siege of Sebastopol. A drawing from *The Illustrated London News.*

BELOW Huts and warm clothing for the army arrive at last in the winter of 1854–5. One of Simpson's drawings.

job with that of Secretary for the Colonies, and it was to him that the Commander-in-Chief and the forces in the field were ultimately responsible. There was also the Secretary of State *at* War, who was Sidney Herbert. His was the financial, as distinct from the operational, responsibility. Which of these two masters directed the army's medical services seems to have been in some doubt; as in many other matters, command was divided; but Sidney Herbert shouldered the responsibility. The set-up would have been ludicrous if it had not been tragic.

If the Director General of the Army Medical department wished to furnish our hospitals in the East some kind of supplies, for instance wine, sago or arrowroot [wrote Kinglake, the historian of the Crimea], he had to send his purpose revolving in an orrery of official bodies, passing from his office at the Horse Guards to Ordnance department, by a leisurely progression to the Admiralty, in good time to the Transport Office, and eventually, if the requisition did not get mislaid on the way, to the shipowners who had to be individually invited to stow the goods in the holds of their vessels, when one should be going in the right direction.

The wonder was not that the hospitals were ill-equipped but that anything ever arrived at all.

For the predictable chaos resulting from this state of affairs Sidney Herbert took the blame; and he took action to meet the disaster. He wrote to Florence: 'There is but one person in England that I know of who would be capable of organizing and superintending such a scheme' – a scheme to send a party of female nurses to Scutari. 'Would you listen to the request and go and superintend the whole thing?' This letter, written on 15 October 1854, crossed one from Florence to Liz Herbert written the day before.

A small private expedition of nurses has been organized for Scutari, and I have been asked to command it [Florence told Liz Herbert]. I take myself out and one nurse. Lady Maria Forester has given £200 to take out three others. We feed and lodge ourselves there, and are to be no expense whatever to the country. . . . I do not say that I believe the *Times* accounts, but I do believe that we may be of use to the wounded wretches.

What did Mr Herbert say to this? Would he give authority and advice? And would Liz write to Lady Stratford, wife of the British Ambassador in Constantinople, to say 'This is not a lady but a real Hospital Nurse? And she has had experience.' And this woman of thirty-four, 'a real Hospital Nurse' and in charge of a London nursing-home, found it natural to add: 'My uncle went down this morning to ask my father and mother's consent.' That battle, at least, had been won; she got the consent, though only after the Government had given her not merely approval but official status, and after Florence's faithful friends the Bracebridges, at a few days' notice, abandoned their congenial life in Warwickshire to grapple at her side with the chaos at Scutari.

Sidney Herbert's decision to offer Florence an official appointment as 'Superintendent of the Female Nursing Establishment of the English General Hospitals in Turkey' was a brave one. No woman had pre-viously been employed to nurse wounded soldiers, and the deepest preju-dices were certain to be aroused. War and medicine, above all else, were jealously-guarded male preserves. For a woman to meddle in both at once, and with government approval, could only cause outrage and resentment. Supported by the Duke of Newcastle, Sidney Herbert secured the Cabinet's agreement to the appointment on 18 October. She was to have complete authority over the selection, disposition and welfare of the nurses, but to act under the orders of the Chief Medical Officer on the spot, Dr Menzies. Directions would be immediately given to the Ambassador, Lord Stratford de Redcliffe, to afford her 'every facility and assistance', and to Dr Menzies to give her 'every aid in his power and every support in the execution of your arduous duties'. The passages and salaries of the nurses would be paid by the Government, who were to start Miss Nightingale off with £1,000 for expenses, after which she would draw on the Purveyor to the Forces at Scutari. Finally, she was to take the greatest care that none of her nurses would 'make use of their position to tamper with or disturb the religious opinions of the patients of any denomination whatever'.

Forty nurses, Sidney Herbert decided, were to go. An office was opened at the Herberts' house in Belgrave Square to receive applications. Far from a flood of eager volunteers, only a trickle came, and these mostly of a type which made those signing them on – Liz Herbert, Mary Stanley and two other ladies – 'ashamed to have [them] in the house. . . . One alone expressed a wish to go from a good motive. Money was the only inducement.' The money was not exactly lavish: up to a shilling a day to start with, plus board and lodgings and a uniform, rising to eighteen to twenty shillings a week after a year's good service. A strict code of discipline was laid down. Nurses might not go out alone or even in pairs; they must be accompanied by the housekeeper or by three other nurses; misbehaviour with soldiers would bring instant dismissal and a third-class passage home. No coloured ribbons on their attire, and liquor to be strictly rationed, a pint of ale or porter for dinner and half a pint for supper, or one ounce of brandy. Thirteen years later Florence wrote, 'As to that stuff about the "enthusiasm" of the nursing in the Crimean campaign – that is all bosh; we had, unfortunately for us, scarcely one woman sent out who was even up to the level of a head nurse.' Instead of forty, only fourteen women with experience in hospitals who, by stretching a good many points, could be considered possible, were found. In this predicament, religious bodies were approached.

Nurses must be selected, Florence wrote, 'with a view to fitness and without reference to religious creed whether Roman Catholic nuns, Dissenting Deaconesses, Protestant Hospital nurses or Anglican sisters'. Approaches were made to the Roman Catholics, to two High Anglican sisterhoods and to one Evangelical body, which refused to co-operate. Thanks to Cardinal Manning's influence, the Roman Catholics agreed to send five nuns from a convent in Bermondsey and five from an orphanage in Norwood. One of the Anglican sisterhoods, founded by Miss Sellon in Devonport, sent eight sisters, and the other, St John's House in Blandford Square, provided six. That brought the total up to thirty-eight but upset the sectarian balance: no less than twenty-four were either Roman Catholics or High Anglicans. No out-and-out Protestants were of the party. Some of the fourteen so-called professional nurses might, so far as anyone could tell, be of that persuasion, but it was remarked by Mary Mohl that the worship of Bacchus was probably more in their line. This preponderance of non-Protestants caused some trouble at the time and much more later on.

Mrs Barnes, a nurse who spent twenty-two years in the field. The photograph was taken in about 1860.

On 21 October 1854, only four days after Sidney Herbert's letter of appointment, Florence, with her thirty-eight ill-assorted nurses in their hastily-made (and ill-fitting and ugly) uniforms, the housekeeper Mrs Clarke and the two devoted Bracebridges, left London for Scutari by way of Boulogne, Paris and Marseilles. Before leaving, the Director of the Army Medical Service, Dr Andrew Smith, assured her that she would find no deficiencies in everything needed for the comfort of the sick and wounded at Scutari. Even Sidney Herbert believed supplies to be adequate; medical stores had been sent out 'in profusion; lint by the *ton* weight, fifteen thousand pairs of sheets, medicine, wine, arrowroot in the same proportion'; and fresh stores were arriving all the time. As to surgeons, there was one to every ninety-five men, the highest proportion ever attained by a British army in the field. Florence preferred to be on the safe side. The *Times* fund had grown to a generous size, and Mr Macdonald accompanied the expedition to supervise its distribution. In Marseilles she invested some of this money, together with some of her own, in supplies she thought might be needed, including, with notable prescience, some portable stoves.

Florence displayed immediately that first quality of a good commander: care for those under command. In Paris, on a Friday, she procured eggs for the Catholic nuns to replace the meat put before them; on arrival in Marseilles she went out to buy them all warm shoes. The 'rough hospital nurses' were flabbergasted; they exclaimed to Uncle Sam Smith, who accompanied the party as far as Marseilles: 'We never had so much care taken of our comforts before; it is not people's way with *us*; we had no notion Miss N would slave herself for us.' 'She looked so calm and noble in it all,' wrote her uncle. She had taken in her pocket-book three letters: one from Fanny, at last giving her blessing; one from Cardinal Manning commending her to God; and one from Richard Monckton Milnes. 'I cannot forget how you went to the East once before, and here am I writing quietly to you about what you are about to do now. You can undertake *that* when you could not undertake me. God bless you, dear Friend, wherever you go.'

She had need of all his blessing. The *Vectis*, in which the party sailed on 27 October 1854, was a most uncomfortable vessel, infested with

OPPOSITE Factory girls making lint to be sent out to the army in the Crimea. This drawing appeared in *The Illustrated London News*.

cockroaches; they ran into a gale so severe that her guns had to be jettisoned, and Florence was prostrated by sea-sickness. On 4 November the *Vectis* anchored in a heavy rainstorm off the Golden Horn. On the opposite shore rose an enormous, ugly, square, yellow building with a tower at each corner, dominating the scruffy little village of Scutari. This was the Turkish army barracks, now the Barrack Hospital where her work was to lie. Its harsh and prison-like exterior cannot have encouraged her. When the Secretary of the Embassy came out to convey an official welcome, he found her stretched on a sofa still too unwell to stand.

The state of the Barrack Hospital was far worse even than she had supposed. So was the enormous weight of prejudice against a woman butting in to men's affairs, especially when a shocking state of inefficiency and neglect was bound to be revealed. Then there were difficulties among her own women, the drunken nurses so undisciplined and the nuns so strange to the life they were now called upon to lead. On top of everything else, the battle of Balaclava had been fought ten days before, and the wounded were starting to come in.

. On the afternoon of their arrival, the nurses were lowered into painted *caiques* and rowed across the Bosporus. The rain had ceased, but there was mud everywhere and the bloated carcase of a horse, worried by a pack of starving dogs, was being washed up and down on the shore. In long skirts and habits, umbrellas in hand, the nurses made their way to the gateway of the grim building. Dr Menzies, the medical officer in charge, and Major Sillery, the Military Commandant, were waiting to receive them. They were shown to their quarters. One room was allocated to the fourteen hospital nurses, another smaller one to the ten nuns, a tiny room, ten feet by ten, to Florence sharing with Selina, and another to serve as sitting-room, office and Mr Bracebridge's bedroom. On a corridor above, a further room was occupied by the eight 'Sellon sisters' – but only after the dead body of a Russian general had been removed, leaving the floor littered with his white hairs. It had a splendid view but practically no furniture, like the rest of the rooms. In the whole hospital there were no tables, not even one for operations. There was nothing to cook with and a daily allowance of water for all purposes of one pint a head. The whole place was filthy, dilapidated and verminous, the central yard a sea of refuse-littered mud. There were rats everywhere; the privies in the towers were stopped up; the walls streamed with damp. The place stank. In the cellars beneath was a scene worthy of some medieval vision of Inferno. More than two hundred women had taken up their quarters, some of them prostitutes, all of them filthy and often drunk, giving birth to babies, starving, quarrelling and dying of cholera.

The doctors were under orders to admit the nurses to the hospital but not to employ their services when there. The authority of the doctors was absolute, and to start with they simply boycotted the Lady Superinten-dent and her women. A single false step on her part would have ruined all chances of success. Florence kept her head and her temper. She set her women to work on sorting out what linen there was and making pillows, stump-rests and slings, while suffering and dying men went untended. Her nurses were restive, but she was firm. No nurse was to set foot in a ward until a doctor invited her.

For four days no invitation came, while the Balaclava wounded poured into the Barracks which were already full. Debarred from entering the wards, Florence turned her attention to the feeding arrange-

Balaclava: sick and wounded soldiers, arriving at the harbour in litters, are transferred to boats for the crossing to Scutari.

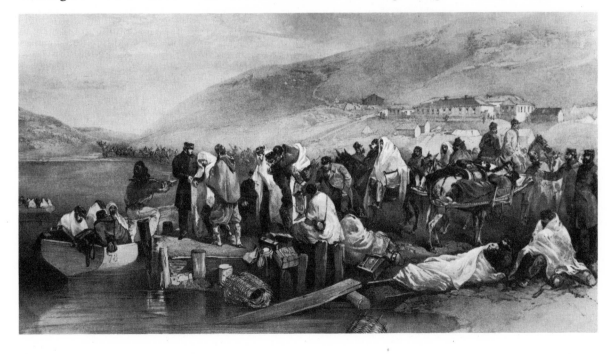

ments. Many of the wounded and sick were literally starving, and others were being killed by trying to eat ill-cooked solids when they should have been on an invalid diet. Such things as arrowroot, wine, milk, jellies and so on simply did not exist. Even if they did, everything had to be obtained through a requisition, signed by two doctors, to the Purveyor, whose staff consisted of two inexperienced clerks. The Purveyor was not even master in his own house; his responsibilities were shared with the Commissariat, who actually bought the goods and made the contracts.

So no one knew exactly who was responsible for what. Opportunities for buckpassing were infinite and well taken. A doctor, having made a requisition, had no power to see that the Purveyor carried it out. It was little wonder that men supposed to be on a liquid diet never saw their arrowroot, sago and wine.

Even the less serious cases were little better off. The Barrack Hospital, supposed to accommodate up to 2,500 patients, had only one kitchen with thirteen coppers in which everything had to be cooked, and tea made; there was no time, or inclination, for keeping them clean. The orderlies stood in line to receive rations from the Purveyor. Mostly these consisted of meat, issued on the bone with everything, gristle, fat and offal, all together. The orderlies hacked it into chunks and threw it into the coppers, each man attaching to his portion some distinguishing mark such as a bit of rag, a button, even a rusty nail. The water was seldom boiling. When the cooks thought enough time had elapsed, they put out the fires and each orderly withdrew his bundle. Meat that had gone in first might be stewed into shreds and later additions virtually raw.

Whether a patient got a hunk of flesh or a bit of bone and gristle was a matter of luck, and often of favouritism. In any case, it was cold; there were no knives and forks, and the men tore at it with their fingers. If they could not eat it, the orderlies gobbled it up – one of the nurses saw an orderly wolf down eight dinners. There were no vegetables, no soups, no puddings. This was the diet on which men suffering from cholera and dysentery, as well as the wounded, were supposed to live. Many of them not only died but died in agonies which could have been avoided.

If no nurse could enter the wards except at the request of a doctor, she could enter the kitchen. Florence had brought stores from Marseilles, including the portable stoves, and Mr Macdonald had plenty of *Times* money to spend in Constantinople. She started to buy and then prepare invalid foods: arrowroot, beef-essence and so on. But nothing could be given to a patient without a written order from a doctor which had to be countersigned by a staff surgeon, who often could not be found.

The filth was beyond description. Under the building were stagnant sewers 'through which the wind blew sewer air up the pipes of numerous open privies into the corridors and wards'. As the privies were choked, large open tubs stood in the wards to receive the ordure. Twenty chamber-pots to serve the needs of a thousand men with dysentery and cholera were, at one time, all that were available. After the nurses were admitted to the wards, Florence herself stood over these tubs and in her quiet, authoritative voice – Mr Bracebridge said that he never heard her raise it – persuaded, for she had no right to command, the orderlies to carry out these tubs, slung between them on a pole, to empty them. As to smells, she told a subsequent Royal Commission that she was well acquainted with the slums of Europe's great cities, but had 'never been in any atmosphere which I could compare with it'.

The woodwork was so rotten that it could not be scrubbed and was saturated with filth, a paradise for vermin and germs. Maggots thrived in the wounds. There were scarcely any blankets and the soldiers lay in their filthy shirts which they would not part with; even if a man 'got one in exchange, he would probably find it full of another man's lice and he preferred to keep his own'. Yet six hundred hospital dresses had but recently arrived, according to a three-man Commission sent out by Sidney Herbert to find out what had gone wrong. 'Neither these dresses, not flannel waistcoats, nor any articles of hospital clothing, were ever issued.'

It was the arrival of casualties from the battle of Balaclava, fought on 25 October 1854, followed by the repulse of the Russian attack at Inkerman on 5 November, that broke the doctors' resistance to 'the Bird' and her flock at Scutari. The trickle of sick and wounded became a flood. These men had endured already perhaps eight or nine days' passage from the Crimean peninsula in ill-equipped vessels, rolling about the open decks often without drugs, dressings or even blankets. Then

A cartoon from *Punch* depicting 'the Bird' and one of her ministering angels tending wounded soldiers in the Crimea.

came the further ordeal of crossing the Bosporus in Turkish *caiques*, and being roughly carried from the shore to be dumped down in the stinking corridors of the two hospitals at Scutari, the General and the much larger Barracks. The cold, wet winter had set in and there was no heating. The doctors turned to any help they could get, even from the disapproved-of women, and soon Florence and her team were at work in the wards. On 14 November 1854 she wrote to a doctor friend:

We had but half an hour's notice before they began landing the wounded. Between one and nine o'clock we had the mattresses stuffed, sewn up, laid down – alas! only upon matting on the floor – the men washed and put to bed, and their wounds dressed . . . twenty-four cases died on the day of landing. The dysentery cases have died at the rate of one in two. Then the day of operations follows. . . .

Despite her chilly welcome by the medical officers, Florence bore them no ill-will; she kept on good terms with them personally, and understood that they were in the grip of a military system they could not ignore or defy. Nothing could be done without an order from a superior officer, the regulations had at all costs to be obeyed, and initiative might well be punished by court-martial. She wrote home on 14 November:

We are very lucky in our Medical Heads. Two of them are brutes and four are angels – for this is a work which makes either angels or devils of men and women too. As for the assistants, they are all Cubs, and will, while a man is breathing his last breath under the knife, lament the 'annoyance of being called up from their dinners by such a fresh influx of wounded'! But unlicked Cubs grow up into good old Bears, tho' I don't know how; for certain it is that the old Bears are good. We have now *four miles* of Beds, and not eighteen inches apart. . . .

As I went my night-rounds among the newly-wounded that first night, there was not one murmur, not one groan, the strictest discipline – the most absolute silence and quiet prevailed – only the steps of the Sentry – I heard one man say, 'I was dreaming of my friends at Home,' and another said, 'I was thinking of them.' These poor fellows bear pain and mutilation with an unshrinking heroism which is really superhuman, and die, or are cut up without a complaint.

No wonder she added: 'Let no lady come out here who is not used to fatigue and privation' – and lacks a strong stomach. Operations were performed in the wards then and there as the men were carried in.

One poor fellow exhausted with haemorrhage has his leg amputated as a last hope, and dies ten minutes after the surgeon has left him. Almost before the breath has left his body, it is sewn up in a blanket and carried away and buried on the same day. We have no room for Corpses in the Wards. . . . Among these exhausted Frames the mortality of the operations is frightful. We have Erysipelas (fever and gangrene), and the Russian wounded are the worst.

Yet Florence was serene – she was in action and at full stretch as she had always wanted. 'We are getting on nicely though in other ways. The Senior Chaplain is a sensible man.' Mrs Roberts of St Thomas's was worth her weight in gold and Mrs Drake a treasure. In other nurses, the dross was more in evidence. In the midst of all this horror, Mrs Lawfield burst out to the Superintendent: 'I came out ma'am, prepared to submit to everything, to be put upon in every way. But there are some things, ma'am, one can't submit to. There is the Caps, ma'am, that suits one face, and some that suits another. And if I'd known, ma'am, about the

Caps, great as was my desire to come out to nurse at Scutari, I wouldn't have come, ma'am.' Florence had already had to send one nurse home, and now four more, all from St John's House, fell out because they would not submit to her strict discipline. Her dwindling team of women was, she wrote, more difficult to manage than four thousand men.

No wonder, then, that another batch of untrained, undisciplined would-be nurses, not even under her authority and rent by class and sectarian divisions, was the last complication she wanted to see. She had taken the precaution of securing, before she left London, a written promise from Sidney Herbert that 'no additional nurses will be sent out to Miss Nightingale until she shall have written home from Scutari and reported how far her labours have been successful, and what number and description of persons, if any, she requires in addition. . . . No one can be sent out until we hear from Miss Nightingale that they are required.' No promise could have been clearer. It was therefore with shock and dismay that she learned, in December 1854, that a party of forty-six women led by her former friend Mary Stanley, who had no nursing experience, was actually on the way.

She was appalled. To begin with, there was nowhere to put them. 'The forty-six', Mr Bracebridge wrote, 'have fallen upon us like a cloud of locusts. Where to house them, where to feed them, place them, is difficult; how to care for them, not to be imagined.' The Principal Medical Officer refused to have anything to do with them. Florence wrote:

I have toiled my way into the confidence of the Medical Men. I have, by incessant vigilance, day and night, introduced something like system into the disorderly operations of these women. And the plan may be said to have succeeded in some measure, *as it stands*. . . . But to have women scampering about the wards of a Military Hospital all day long, which they would do, did an increased number relax the discipline and increase their leisure, would be as improper as absurd.

And then she rounded on Sidney Herbert. 'You have sacrificed a cause so near my heart. You have sacrificed your own written word to a popular cry. You must feel that I ought to resign . . . and I only remain at my post till I have provided in some measure for these poor wanderers.'

OPPOSITE A photograph of Florence. She disliked having her photograph taken, but those that survive confirm reports of her attractive looks.

Four days before Florence reached Scutari, there had arrived a friend of Sidney Herbert's, an energetic clergyman, the Reverend Sidney Godolphin Osborne, who had come out to help the hospital chaplain but soon found himself helping surgeons to amputate and orderlies to dress wounds as well. His angry reports to *The Times* supplemented Russell's, and stoked the fires of public indignation. He was wholeheartedly on Florence's side, and wrote of her 'wonderful power to command help, and quickness to see where it would most avail'. Had it not been for Florence and her nurses and for Mr Macdonald and his fund, he did not see how a total breakdown could have been avoided after the battle of Inkerman. He wrote to Sidney Herbert: 'As to Miss Nightingale and her companions, nothing can be said too strong in their praise; she works them wonderfully, and they are so useful that I have no hesitation in saying that some twenty more of the same sort would be a very great blessing to the establishment. . . .'

Others were of the same opinion. Cardinal Manning, anxious to send out more nuns, encouraged Mary Stanley, the Dean of Westminster's sister, who had strong Catholic leanings, to head the party. Herbert was hard-pressed, over-worked and grappling with a virtual collapse of the logistics of the Crimean army, and the question of nurses at Scutari, where the experiment seemed to be going well, was only one of very many. He gave permission and the nurses sailed.

Nurses, one might say, in name only. Mary Stanley's party was divided into ladies (nine), Catholic Sisters of Mercy (fifteen) and paid nurses (twenty-two). The ladies were most reluctant to mix with the paid nurses, who shocked them *en route* by swearing, getting drunk and objecting to French food. One of them, Jane Evans, was more at home with animal than human patients, having spent her life tending pigs and cows. Another, Elizabeth Davis (born Cadwaladyr) was a wild Welsh woman who had roamed the world in domestic service and wrote: 'I did not like the name of Nightingale' – nor the person, when they met. Mary Stanley was in the throes of a religious crisis, had no experience of controlling others and had made no plans. When they reached Scutari on 17 December 1854, Mr Bracebridge broke it to them that they must go on to Therapia, about fifteen miles away, where the Ambassador had

A group of British soldiers
fighting the cold of the
Crimea in their winter
uniform. Frostbite was an
ever-present risk. The
photograph is by Fenton.

put his summer villa at their disposal. With them were a clergyman and a Member of Parliament, whom Florence interviewed in her least melting mood. She disclaimed all responsibility for the party and sent the two gentlemen off with fleas in their ears. A few days later they were back, asking for succour; all the money they had brought was gone and they were virtually destitute. Florence loaned Mary Stanley £90 immediately from her own pocket, and subsequently another £300.

Meanwhile, sick men were pouring in from the mud-bound, icy camp near Balaclava, where cholera had broken out again and men were going down on all sides with frostbite, dysentery and sheer exhaustion. A disastrous hurricane on 14 November had sunk two transports loaded with anxiously-awaited supplies, including those for the hospitals, and almost all the warm winter clothing. As to the town itself, reported Russell, 'words cannot describe its filth, its horrors, its hospitals, its burials, its dead and dying Turks, its crowded lanes, its noisome sheds, its beastly purlieus, or its decay'. Regiments were reduced in strength to a few dozen men; 'The 63rd Regiment may almost be said to have disappeared.' At Scutari, Florence, Mr Bracebridge wrote, 'was working herself to death; never sits down to breakfast or dinner without interruption, often never dines . . . the attempt to do more will kill her . . . today, two hundred sick landed looking worse than any others yet'.

There were four miles of corridor at the Barrack Hospital crammed with patients, and every night Florence went the rounds to bring the sick and wounded comfort, carrying a Turkish lantern consisting of a single candle inside a circular collapsible shade. So was born the legend of 'the Lady with a Lamp' – unlike many legends, one not so far from the truth. The phrase was later coined by Longfellow in his famous verse:

> Lo! in that hour of misery
> A lady with a lamp I see
>   Pass through the glimmering gloom,
>   And flit from room to room.
> And slow, as in a dream of bliss
> The speechless sufferer turns to kiss
>   Her shadow, as it falls
>   Upon the darkening walls.

A more prosaic eye-witness account of the nightly parade was given by Fanny Taylor, one of Mary Stanley's 'ladies' – a description on which Longfellow may have drawn:

It seemed an endless walk and was not easily forgotten. As we slowly passed along, the silence was profound; very seldom did a moan or cry from those multitudes of deeply suffering ones fall on our ears. A dim light burnt here and there. Miss Nightingale carried her lantern, which she would set down before she bent over any of the patients. I much admired Miss Nightingale's manner to the men – it was so tender and kind. . . . The hospital was crowded to its fullest extent. The building, which has since been reckoned to hold, with comfort, seventeen hundred men, then held between three and four thousand. Miss Nightingale assigned me my work. . . .

With 'another lady and one nurse' she was to look after fifteen hundred patients. (There were, of course, also untrained orderlies.) The Stanley party had by then been parcelled out between the various hospitals: a few to Scutari, others, under Mary Stanley herself, to a military hospital newly opened at Koulali, seven to Balaclava and three straight home again, two of them 'from their habits of intoxication'. At night the nurses lay down, Miss Taylor said, wearied 'not so much from fatigue, though that was great, as from sickness of heart from living amidst that mass of hopeless suffering'.

The suffering was not diminished when the deputy Inspector General of the Medical Services issued an order forbidding any cooking in the wards. Florence's nurses had been making beef-tea on portable stoves. 'It was very hard after Dr Cummings's order had been issued,' Miss Taylor wrote, 'to pace the corridor and hear perhaps the low voice of a fever patient, "Give me a drink for the love of God", and have none to give. . . . In all the confusion and distress of Scutari hospital, military discipline was never lost sight of, and an infringement of its smallest observance was worse than letting twenty men die from neglect.' No wonder that between fifty and seventy a day were being buried on the cliff-side – one hundred during Christmas week.

One of the Turkish lamps that belonged to Florence and around which the legend of 'the Lady with a Lamp' was built. She actually owned at least two lamps of this sort.

Calamity
Unparalleled

CHAPTER FOUR

CALAMITY UNPARALLELED

A drawing from a medical textbook of the 1850s illustrating the administration of chloroform as an anaesthetic.
PREVIOUS PAGES Officers and soldiers of the 4th Dragoons entertain some of their French allies in the Light Cavalry Camp before Sebastopol. One of the soldiers' wives stands in the foreground. The photograph is by Fenton.
OPPOSITE (TOP) Balaclava Harbour and Town: a watercolour by Captain H. A. Williamson.
(BOTTOM) The church of Kadikoi at Balaclava, which was used as a hospital by British troops in the winter of 1854–5. Drawn by W. G. Cattermole.

THE MAN RESPONSIBLE for the British army medical services in this campaign was Dr John Hall, aged sixty-three. He had been summoned from Bombay and, after a single visit to Scutari in October 1854, reported that 'the whole hospital establishment here is on a very creditable footing and nothing is lacking'. If such complacency seems hard to credit, it may be said that older men used older standards of comparison, mainly those of the Peninsula War. When Sir George Brown, commander of the Light Brigade in the Crimea, had been wounded in both legs forty years before in Spain, he had been thrown into a cart and left to fare as best he might; he thought carts perfectly adequate and 'hates ambulances as the invention of the Evil One'.

Dr Hall was of this kidney. (Florence called him 'a fossil of the pure Red Sandstone'.) Chloroform was coming into general use, but he advised his officers that 'the smart use of the knife is a powerful stimulant and it is much better to hear a man bawl lustily than to see him sink silently into the grave'. (Most of his officers ignored this advice – it was not an order – and at Scutari chloroform was nearly always used, by holding a saturated handkerchief over the man's face.) Dr Hall's opinion of women nurses in military hospitals can be surmised from his observation to his superior, Dr Andrew Smith, that the Government had sent out 'pathologists, sanitary commissioners, and I don't know what 'issioners, with high salaries and no occupation. Then we have female Inspectors and Directors of Nurses, and I don't know what besides.'

92

MISS
NIGHTINGALE

Dr Hall was a martinet, and his staff were too much in awe of him to question his views. Once committed to the proposition that all was for the best in the best of all possible worlds at Scutari, no one under his authority dared to contradict him, and officials like the Ambassador were only too glad to accept his word. In over two years Lord Stratford de Redcliffe paid only one brief visit to the Scutari hospital (he was said to travel with twenty-five servants and seventy tons of plate), and then suggested that, as the hospitals had all they needed, The *Times* fund should be devoted to building an Anglican church in Constantinople. Dr Hall was Florence's real enemy in the Crimean campaign. He was not at Scutari but at Balaclava, and left the conduct of Scutari matters to the Principal Medical Officer, Dr Menzies, who was not himself ill-disposed, but did not dare to go against his superior.

Dr Hall was a conscientious and hard-working officer who did not reach the Crimea until three months before the battle for the Alma. He had therefore had no say in the organization, or lack of it, of the medical arrangements for the expeditionary force. Nor could the confusion which arose at Varna when the army was shipped across the Black Sea be laid at his door. In this lay the seeds of all the trouble: in particular, the order that the men should leave behind their knapsacks, and the loss of forage for the baggage animals, which condemned the army to a crippling shortage of transport. It was hardly his fault, for instance, that the captain of the *Andes*, one of two vessels earmarked for the transport of medical supplies and ambulance carts to Scutari, stowed them in the hold and disclaimed all knowledge of them; months later they came to light in a store at Balaclava, broken into and plundered.

Florence had allies as well as enemies among the doctors. One was Dr McGrigor. He backed her determination to repair a part of the Barracks building so dilapidated that it was not in use as a hospital, although it would accommodate another eight hundred men. Despite an order from the Commander-in-Chief, no branch of the army seemed willing to incur the expense. Florence appealed, through Lady Stratford, to the Ambassador, and work was begun. The Turkish workmen struck for higher pay. The Ambassador said it was no affair of his. Florence engaged more workmen – two hundred instead of 124 – and paid them

OPPOSITE Queen Victoria receiving wounded soldiers from the Crimea, an engraving after the painting by Barrett. She did much to raise morale among her soldiers, sending messages and gifts out to the Crimea, though Florence must have had as much difficulty in dispensing the Queen's gifts as she did with the many others that poured in.

PREVIOUS PAGES (LEFT) *The Welcome Arrival*: an oil painting by D. Luard. Officers open parcels sent out to them by their families.
(RIGHT) A porcelain model of Florence with a wounded soldier. These figures became common in Victorian England as the legend of 'the Lady with a Lamp' was established.

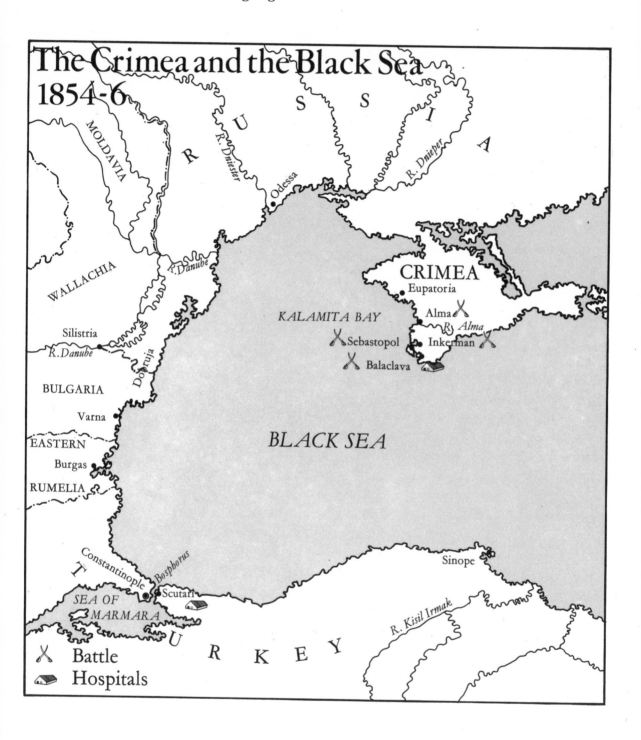

The Crimea and the Black Sea
1854-6

MOLDAVIA

R U S S I A

R. Dniester

R. Dnieper

Odessa

WALLACHIA

R. Danube

CRIMEA

Eupatoria

KALAMITA BAY

Alma

R. Alma

Silistria

Sebastopol

Inkerman

R. Danube

Dobruja

Balaclava

BULGARIA

Varna

BLACK SEA

EASTERN

Burgas

RUMELIA

Constantinople

Bosphorus

Sinope

T

Scutari

SEA OF
MARMARA

R. Kisil Irmak

U   R   K   E   Y

✗ Battle
🏠 Hospitals

herself, partly out of her own pocket and partly from the *Times* fund. The repairs were completed, and new wards equipped in time to receive two ship-loads of 'frost-bitten, demi-nude, starved, ragged men' on 19 January 1855.

Frostbitten soldiers escorted to Balaclava on horseback. Drawn by an artist for *The Illustrated London News.*

Sometimes Dr McGrigor went too far. When, in March 1855, a quantity of bedding and utensils arrived, he had them immediately installed in the wards. But they had not been through the proper channels and Dr Cummings ordered them to be removed. As one of the doctors said to Florence: 'It is not a question of efficiency, nor of the comfort of the patient, but of the Regulations of the Service.' The new Military Commandant, Lord William Paulet, was no help at all. He saw the evils, Florence wrote, but then 'shuts his eyes and hopes when he opens them he shall see something else'. Meanwhile he went picnicking with Lady Stratford and others of the Embassy staff on the shores of the Bosporus.

To keep her temper and her purpose in the face of all this inefficiency, timidity and intrigue, and when she herself was subject to such extremes of fatigue, must have required almost superhuman self-control. 'What

A cartoon depicting the chaos that reigned in the storehouse at Scutari. Florence stands surrounded by it all.

I have done I shall continue doing,' she wrote, '. . . but I am weary of this hopeless work.' Never had she felt so alone. Her one true friend and ally, despite a 'betrayal' to which she over-reacted and which she quickly forgave, was three thousand miles away in London. Sidney Herbert's support never wavered. To every one of her requests he responded, but he was himself a prisoner of the system and could only express wishes which others might, or might not, carry out. He wrote to Dr Cumming,

that all agreed on the excellency of the medical men; it was organization that was wanted. Stores are sent but cannot be found, or if found are not used, because no one knows whose business it is to open them. I earnestly hope that now you are arrived you will introduce order and method. . . . Let all offers of supplies be accepted if they are wanted, the first thing is that the sick should not want.

And again to Dr Cumming: 'Pray recollect in your demands upon us here . . . that there is no question of pounds, shillings and pence in such matters, but whatever can be got *must* be got.' This staggered the Purveyor, Mr Wreford, who exclaimed: 'This is the first time I have had it in writing that I was not to spare expense. I never knew that I might not be thrown overboard.' (It seems impossible, Sidney Herbert wrote of Mr Wreford, 'to make him understand that the business of a purveyor is to purvey'.)

I am a kind of General Dealer [Florence wrote in January 1855], in socks, shirts, knives and forks, wooden spoons, tin baths, tables and forms, cabbages and carrots, operating tables, towels and soap, small toothcombs, scissors, bedpans and stump pillows. I will send you a picture of my Caravanserai, into which beasts come in and out. Indeed the vermin might, if they had but 'unity of purpose', carry off the four miles of beds on their backs, and march with them into the War Office, Horse Guards, s w.

The Caravanserai was the 'extra-diet' kitchen from which invalid foods were issued on the doctors' orders. It was in continual use. Then there were stores from which she issued everything imaginable – shirts, flannel, kettles, saucepans, socks, scrubbing brushes, combs – either bought by the invaluable Mr Macdonald or sent direct to her by well-wishers in Britain. All these things the Purveyor should have provided. He did not. On one occasion Florence knew that twenty-seven thousand shirts had been landed at Scutari. The Purveyor would not release them until authorized to do so by a Board of Survey, and the Board did not meet for another three weeks. Meanwhile the men shivered. From her own stores, fifty-thousand shirts were issued. As the winter went on, scurvy became rife. Two consignments of fresh vegetables were actually thrown into the harbour at Balaclava because of a confusion as to whom they were consigned. One of the activities Florence organized was the washing, which had been put out to contract. Much of the bedding was never washed at all, or merely rinsed in cold water to be sent back as verminous as before. Florence took matters into her own hands. She hired a Turkish house, got the army engineers to install boilers and employed the soldiers' wives to do the work. For the first time, the Scutari hospital had clean linen. To Sidney Herbert, Florence continued to pour out in frequent letters her trials and tribulations and her opinion of her colleagues. Sometimes a note of near-hysteria, even

OPPOSITE The washing
establishment at the General
Hospital at Balaclava.
LEFT A drying closet
specially designed for the
hospital at Scutari. It
greatly facilitated the regular
supply of clean linen.

persecution mania, crept in; she was over-tired, over-worked, over-strained and began to look on almost everyone as an enemy, and on all criticism as a stab in the back: 'Among all the men here, is there *one* really anxious for the good of these hospitals, *one* who is not an insincere animal at the bottom, who is not thinking of going in on the winning side? . . . I do believe . . . you and I and Bracebridge are the only ones who really care for them.' In a soothing letter Herbert warned her against exaggeration: 'It is always wise in a public document to understate your case. . . . My moral is that you must write more calmly, and not yourself accuse or attribute motives to those whose mis-statements you may disprove, and whose misconduct you may expose without either, and do it far more effectively too.'

Sound advice, in the calm setting of Parliament and Whitehall in London, but hard to follow when the trenches and redoubts before Sebastopol were so close at hand. The mean strength of the British army in the Crimea in the quarter ending 31 December 1855 was 38,789 and

OPPOSITE Queen
Victoria's first visit to
wounded soldiers who had
been sent back from the
Crimea to the Brompton
Hospital in Chatham.
After a painting by Barrett.

of these 25,336 – not far off three men out of every four – were 'under medical treatment' and unfit for duty. Before the winter was out, thousands more were to die. 'Yesterday and the day before, the frost-bitten men landed from the *Golden Fleece* exceeded in misery anything we have seen – they were all *stretcher cases*, and the mortality is frightful, thirty in the last twenty-four hours in this hospital alone. One day last week it was forty, and the number of burials from the Scutari hospitals seventy-two. We bury every twenty-four hours.'

One of Florence's nurses was Sister Margaret Goodman, a Sellonite or 'Protestant nun'. She wrote:

The patients were so emaciated, that after any length of time spent on the straw beds it was very difficult to prevent the skin on their back and hip from rubbing off... the constant pressure and rubbing prevented the new skin from growing. ... The agonies of one man who was brought in after a stormy passage were most fearful to witness. The doctor proceeded to take off the bandages which enveloped the part from which his leg had been cut off, but he cried, 'Not there, it is my back.' ... His whole back, together with his two shoulders, and even the back of his head were divested of skin: he lingered but a few weeks.

In these circumstances over-statements would seem hard to make; and a lack of calmness, a note of near-hysteria, a tendency to lash out at those in high places was, to say the least, understandable.

But one, at least, of those in high places was deeply moved by such reports. These sick and dying men were the Queen's men and at least she could assure them that she was not indifferent to their sufferings. On 6 December she wrote to Sidney Herbert telling him to

Let Mrs Herbert know that I wish Miss Nightingale and the ladies would tell these poor noble wounded and sick men that *no one* takes a warmer interest or feels more for their sufferings or admires their courage and heroism *more* than does their Queen. Day and night she thinks of her beloved troops. So does the Prince. Beg Mrs Herbert to communicate these my words to those ladies, as I know *our* sympathy is valued by these noble fellows.

The message was read aloud in the wards at Scutari and the Queen was right, the men were touched. 'It is a very feeling letter,' one said;

another: 'Queen Victoria is a Queen what is very *fond* of her soldiers.' She also sent them gifts to be distributed by Florence, with a message that Miss Nightingale's 'soothing attendance upon these wounded and sick soldiers had been observed by the Queen with sentiments of the highest approval and admiration'. Was there anything the Queen could do personally to reward her sick soldiers? Yes, Florence quickly replied, there was; end the anomaly whereby a sick man's pay was docked 9d a day whereas a wounded man lost only 4½d a day; and obtain from the Sultan of Turkey a *firman* making over the cemetery at Scutari to the British. This seemed little enough, but the Queen acted and both suggestions were carried out.

The year 1855 opened with more men in hospital than there were in the camps before Sebastopol. 'Calamity unparalleled in the history of calamity', Florence wrote. Most of them were sick not wounded men, stricken by malnutrition, scurvy, frost-bite and forms of cholera and dysentery. It spread throughout the wards and soon surgeons, orderlies and nurses were dying – four surgeons in three weeks. Florence's indifference to contagion was absolute. She was everywhere, needing little sleep and no leisure. 'If the soldiers were told that the roof had opened and she had gone up palpably to heaven,' Richard Monckton Milnes commented, 'they would not be least surprised.' The cold that winter was intense, her stove so useless that it was used as an extra table, the ink froze in its well. All day long people besieged her with requests, demands, problems to be solved. All night long, it seemed – it was said that the light in her room was never out – she wrote and wrote and wrote, endless letters, reports, plans for improving the administration of the hospitals and reforming the medical services of the army. And still she went her rounds along the corridors crammed with sick men, speaking to them, touching them, making them as comfortable as she could and helping them to die. She reckoned that she witnessed two thousand deaths that winter.

It was true that some men kissed her shadow as she passed. They also gave up swearing. Despite their pain and misery, they set so strict a guard on their tongues that these wards full of private soldiers became, as one observer noted, 'as holy as a church'. She herself wrote later:

The tears come into my eyes as I think how, amidst scenes of loathsome disease and death, there rose above it all the innate dignity, gentleness and chivalry of the men (for never surely was chivalry so strikingly exemplified) shining in the midst of what must be considered the lowest sinks of human misery, and preventing instinctively the use of one expression which could distress a gentlewoman.

Sectarian disputes, in such a scene, seem at this distance indecently irrelevant, but they persisted like a sharp pebble in Florence's shoe. Her own original party of nurses – Catholics, 'Protestant nuns' (Sellonites) and professionals – were working smoothly together under her unwinking eye. The trouble came from Mary Stanley's party, split between Koulali, the General Hospital at Scutari and the hospitals at Balaclava whither Mother Bridgeman – known to Florence as Mother Brickbat – had taken some of her Catholic nuns.

From the first, Mary Stanley had refused to accept Florence's authority and gone over her head to Dr Cumming, and to the Ambassador, whose kitchens supplied her with appetizing food – she found the ordinary rations uneatable. A priest who had followed her to Scutari was, at this very time, preparing her to be received into the Roman Church. Care of the men's souls was, in her view, at least equal in importance to care of their bodies. From this it was a small step to proselytizing. There were other complaints. One doctor said of the nuns that they were 'inefficient, sombre, and disliked by all'. As for the ladies, Florence in a scathing letter to Sidney Herbert said that they were 'pottering and messing about with little cookeries of individual beef-teas', a different matter from fitting out four extra diet kitchens, organizing laundry and ward equipment and getting down to brass tacks generally as she and her own nurses had done. To Herbert she protested against 'the lady plan':

It ends in nothing but spiritual flirtation between the ladies and the soldiers. I saw enough of that here; it pets the particular man, it gets nothing done in the general. . . . The ladies all quarrel among themselves. The medical men all laugh at their helplessness, but like to have them about for the sake of a little female society, which is natural, but not our object.

If the ladies pottered, all too many of the professionals tippled, including several of Florence's own band. What with drinking, proselytizing and illness, numbers were dwindling and Florence asked Liz Herbert to send out a replacement for Mary Stanley, who wanted to go home, and six more nurses for herself. Protestant if possible, and not overweight. 'Above fourteen stone we will not have; provision of bedsteads is not strong enough.' Three of them had almost swamped a *caique* on the Bosporus; no more 'fat, drunken old dames', she implored. Liz sent out six respectable Presbyterians, but even so, her husband warned Florence that 'she has no confidence in any of them as to drinking, although nothing can exceed the testimonials these have got.'

Florence was never vindictive but she could be harsh in her judgments. Mary Stanley was not strong, she was not a nurse and she had never intended to stay longer at Scutari than was necessary to settle her charges. A party of her ladies went to Balaclava under the leadership of Miss Shaw Stewart, an efficient and hard-working woman and a great admirer of Florence. They made an immediate and favourable impression on the authorities, but Florence continued to resent the posting of nurses to Balaclava without her consent.

Early in February 1855, following a motion moved on 26 January by Mr Roebuck demanding an enquiry into the conduct of Crimean affairs, the Government resigned and Sidney Herbert went out of office. He was replaced by Lord Panmure, a Scot with large estates in Forfarshire who was to become the Earl of Dalhousie. He was a man of some ability and considerable indolence, skilled alike in shooting grouse and catching salmon and in avoiding trouble, and decisions that might lead to trouble, in politics. A large head which he waved from side to side had earned him the name of 'the Bison'. Although he and Florence were strangers to each other, he was a friend of Palmerston's, now Prime Minister and always her ally. Panmure gave her all the support he could without angering the army medical authorities, especially Dr Andrew Smith and Dr Hall who were firmly ensconsed.

One of his first acts as Minister was to appoint a Sanitary Commission to go immediately to the scene in February 1855, not merely to report on the state of the hospitals, but to take immediate action to put matters

OPPOSITE Lord Panmure, 'the Bison'. He was to prove a formidable opponent to Florence's plans to reform the administration of the army. He was a man of strong religious feeling and considerable generosity, the full extent of which was revealed only after his death.

right. Their instructions, drafted in great detail, sounded a most unusual note of urgency. The Commissioners were not only to decide what was wrong and give orders to rectify it but to 'see instantly' that their orders were carried out and to superintend the work day-to-day until it was finished. It was generally believed that Florence herself drafted these instructions, routing them through her old friend Lord Shaftesbury who had proposed and pressed for the Commission's appointment.

This Commission consisted of two doctors and a civil engineer. The senior doctor, John Sutherland, was to remain Florence's adviser, disciple, physician and virtual slave until his death thirty-six years later. He was a Scot, born in Edinburgh in 1808, appointed in 1848 as an inspector under the newly formed General Board of Health, and a pioneer in the relatively new field of public sanitation – or public health, as we should call it today.

The Commissioners reached Scutari in March 1855. True to their instruction, they did not just report, they acted. Under the Barrack Hospital lay an open sewer choked with excrement; they had the sewer cleared and flushed. The hospital walls were cleansed and lime-washed; the wooden platforms used as beds by patients and as dormitories by rats were destroyed; and the water supply, found to be passing over the carcase of a horse and contaminated by choked privies, was put in order. From the courtyard and precincts generally the remains of twenty-six dead animals, plus literally tons of rubbish and filth, were moved. The effect was spectacular. Mortality began at once to fall. There were troubles enough to come. During the winter of 1855-6, in seven months, some ten thousand died, all but twelve hundred cholera victims, from causes in the main preventible. The activities of Dr Sutherland's trio marked the turning of the tide. Thus the Sanitary Commission, in Florence's words, saved the British army in the Crimea.

A stream of commissions, Members of Parliament and official envoys was now arriving. Soon after Dr Sutherland came a two-man Commission to enquire into the state of the Commissariat, in March 1855. Sir John McNeill was summoned from his work on the Board of Supervision for the Relief of the Poor in Scotland to head the enquiry. Also a doctor, he became one of Florence's closest friends. He was now nearly

OPPOSITE Two members of the Sanitary Commission: Dr John Sutherland (left) and Robert Rawlinson (right), a distinguished civil engineer who was subsequently knighted. Both men were also to serve on the Indian Sanitary Commission. Though she rarely acknowledged his help, Florence could not have won half her battles without Sutherland's constant support and hard work.

A French *cantinière* photographed by Fenton. Usually the wife of a French NCO, she was employed to help with the canteen and to give first aid to the injured. The British also took out to the battlefields a select number of wives to help with cooking, laundering and mending clothes. But it was rare for an officer's wife to travel with her husband's regiment, as did Fanny Duberly, author of the bestseller *Journal Kept during the Russian War*.

sixty, a man of great charm, personality, good looks and ability, who had started his career as a surgeon in India and risen to become a diplomat in Persia and an expert on Persian affairs. With him was Colonel Alexander Tulloch, RE.

On the supply side, decided the Commission, the army's most pressing need was for soft bread; the gums of so many men had been rotted by scurvy that they could not eat the hard biscuits. Tulloch had ovens built and organized bakeries. The meat was so salty that some regiments were throwing away fifty to a hundred pounds daily. Nearly twenty thousand pounds of lime juice had reached Balaclava on 10 December and not an ounce had been issued until the following February. Unroasted coffee beans were being issued when 2,705 pounds of tea were lying unopened in the Commissariat's stores. While lack of transport was paralysing the army because the baggage animals were starving, unlimited quantities of straw were to be had all along the shores of the Bosporus, and Mr Filder, the Commissary-General, had at his disposal sixteen ships which had lain idle all the winter.

When their report was presented to Parliament, it created a furore and a demand for immediate action. Instead, a Board composed of seven elderly generals was appointed – the so-called Chelsea Board – to hear the officers' defence. The ranks were closed, the white-wash diligently applied and everyone concerned, instead of being sacked, was promoted, with the sole exception of Mr Filder, who was allowed to resign.

Florence meanwhile, put her own commissariat in order. In March 1855, M Alexis Soyer, chief chef of the Reform Club in London, arrived. In appearance a kind of stage Frenchman – dapper, voluble, stylishly dressed, with a small imperial beard – he had a high, and justified, opinion of his own abilities. At the time of the Irish potato famine he had organized soup-kitchens in Dublin and taught society ladies how to make soup. Now, at Florence's invitation, he travelled to Scutari at his own expense, attended by four cooks and a 'gentleman of colour' as his secretary. In the Barracks Hospital he at once reconditioned the boilers, stopped the practice of throwing away the broth in which the meat had been cooked, trained orderlies as cooks and tried to get the meat boned. In this he failed, for it could not be done without a new Regula-

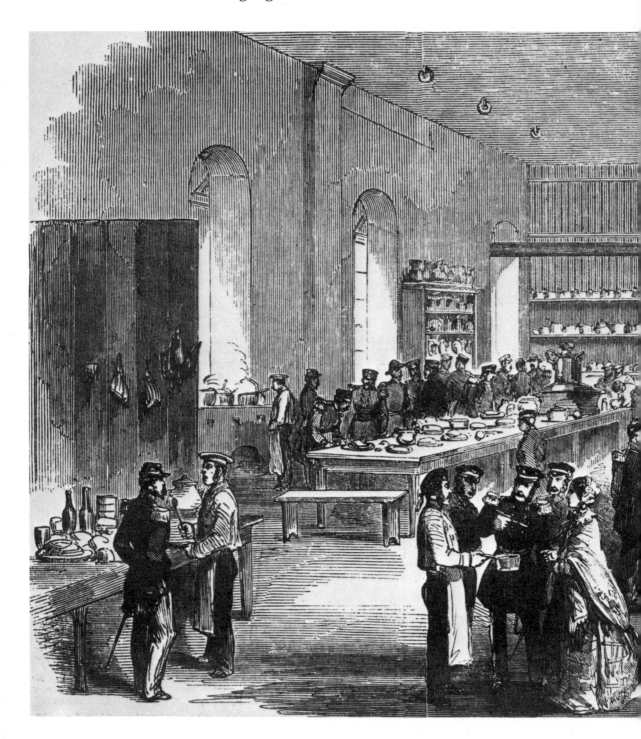

One of Alexis Soyer's kitchens at the Scutari General Hospital. Although accustomed to providing first-class meals for the well-to-do at London's Reform Club, Soyer also had a clear grasp of the principles involved in catering economically for large numbers, most of whom were too sick to manage a normal diet.

Alexis Soyer: an engraving
from a sketch by his wife
Emma. If Florence was
impressed by his culinary
genius, he for his part
became her devoted helper.
Before his premature death
in 1858, he had opened his
model kitchen at
Wellington Barracks.

tion of the Service. Undeterred, he designed new ovens and a teapot that would serve thirty men, and drew up menus from army rations that not only delighted the patients – they cheered him as he passed down the wards – but pleased Lord and Lady Stratford.

By early summer, mortality at the Scutari hospitals had dropped from forty-two to 2·2 per cent. The time had come for a visit to the Crimea, which had four main hospitals, in addition to a number of small field ones. Two of them, the General and the Castle, had accepted women nurses, all of Mary Stanley's party: among them Elizabeth Davis, who was in charge of the extra-diet kitchen at the General Hospital. She herself was being recklessly extravagant, but accused Florence of living on the fat of the land while her nurses went hungry; the superintendent, weak and ineffective Miss Weare, seemed quite unable to control her. Discipline was lax, and the nurses' defiance of Florence's authority was being aided and abetted by Dr Hall and the Purveyor-General, Mr David Fitzgerald. An unfortunate ambiguity in the wording of her instructions gave them their excuse. She had been appointed as 'Superintendent of the Female Nursing Establishment in the English Military General Hospitals in Turkey', and the Crimea was not in Turkey. Therefore, they held, what went on in the Crimean hospitals was no business of hers.

But they could not openly defy her since she had the backing of the Prime Minister, of Lord Panmure and of the Commander-in-Chief, Lord Raglan. Born Lord Fitzroy Somerset, a son of the Duke of Beaufort, Lord Raglan, aged sixty-six, was handsome, charming, magnanimous and brave. He had lost an arm on the field of Waterloo and for over forty years had served the Duke of Wellington as his devoted aide. Lord Raglan's prestige was therefore as immense as his skill as a military commander was meagre. Within a few days of Florence's arrival at Scutari, he had sent her a warmly welcoming letter, and later she was to write gratefully of the support and encouragement he had given her, and of 'the high courtesy and true manliness of his character'. She set out for Balaclava confident that, with this support, she could deal with the lesser fry such as Dr Hall and Mr Fitzgerald, and nurses who were defiant like Mrs Davis or weak like Miss Weare.

A Twelvemonth of Dirt

CHAPTER FIVE

A TWELVEMONTH OF DIRT

FLORENCE REACHED BALACLAVA on 5 May 1855 in the *Robert Lowe*, with a bevy of attendants. There was the faithful Mr Bracebridge, notebook in hand, and Selina; M Soyer, several cooks and his coloured secretary; a young drummer-boy who darted everywhere at her beck and call 'full of activity, wit, intelligence and glee', according to M Soyer, and four nurses including her best one, Mrs Roberts. 'Having been at Scutari six months today,' she wrote to her mother, 'am in sympathy with God, fulfilling the purpose I came into the world for. What the disappointments of the conclusion of these six months are no one can tell. But I am not dead, but alive.'

Very much alive, indeed. Her headquarters on board the *Robert Lowe* were soon thronged with visitors come to pay their respects, among them Sir John McNeill and Colonel Tulloch. Next day she set out, accompanied by her *entourage*, and mounted on 'a very pretty mare of a golden colour', to inspect the hospitals and meet their medical heads; Dr Hall was pointedly absent. She had, M Soyer wrote, quite a martial air, attired in a 'genteel amazone', or riding-habit, instead of her normal plain black or grey woollen dress with a white apron and cap – 'religiously simple and unsophisticated'. Soyer drew the picture of a most attractive woman with blue, sparkling eyes, a small, well-formed mouth and remarkably expressive features: 'One can almost anticipate by her countenance what she is about to say.' In rhapsodizing over the 'gentle smile that passes radiantly over her countenance, thus proving her

PREVIOUS PAGES Florence visting the hut hospitals at Balaclava. It was after this expedition that she who had miraculously resisted all infection for nearly a year succumbed to a fever that almost killed her.

evenness of temper', and averring that 'no member of the fair sex can be more amiable and gentle than Miss Nightingale', he was perhaps giving gallantry its head.

After the hospitals, they visited the trenches before Sebastopol and came within range of enemy fire; a shell whistled over their heads. Taking her hand, M Soyer helped Florence to mount a mortar in a forward battery, inviting her escort to 'behold this amiable lady sitting fearlessly upon that terrible instrument of war'. Russian guns stepped up their cannonade, which 'gave a kind of martial note of approval' to the little charade. A French corporal 'remarked that ladies often came to this spot to get a view, and that he had never known this enemy to fire while they were present'.

A contemporary sketch of the road to Sebastopol, showing the Commissariat waggons and the fascines used to build up fortifications. From *The Illustrated London News*.

Simpson's impression of
the road from Balaclava to
Sebastopol during wet
weather. In such conditions
casualties were inevitable,
even before the men took up
their positions.

A few days later Florence was taken dangerously ill with 'Crimean fever'. She was carried in a stretcher to the Castle Hospital above the town, with Mrs Roberts in attendance and M Soyer's secretary holding a white sunshade over her head. She became delirious, and the doctors did not think she could live. They had not reckoned with her toughness of spirit. She summoned reserves of strength and gradually the fever subsided. Meanwhile the whole of Balaclava, Soyer wrote, was in an uproar as the news spread, and when it reached Scutari, the men turned their faces to the wall and cried.

In her delirium she could not stop writing, writing, writing, endless orders, requisitions, notes. On 24 May 1855 a soldier in a cloak arrived on horseback to see her. Mrs Roberts ordered him back, saying that the patient could not be disturbed, and when he persisted asked 'Pray who are you?' 'Only a soldier,' he replied, 'but I have come a long way to see her and she knows me well.' It was Lord Raglan. He drew up a stool to her bedside, talked to her at length and was able to report to London, where consternation was nationwide, that she was out of danger. A month later he himself was dead.

Florence wanted to stay on in the Crimea; the doctors pressed her to return to England; and a compromise was reached that she should go to Scutari. Lord Ward offered her his steam yacht, but the doctors selected a transport called the *Jura* and she was taken aboard. A large number of horses had just been unloaded, leaving a strong smell; Florence fainted, and was transferred first to a naval vessel and then to Lord Ward's yacht. Some confusion surrounds this episode. Mr Bracebridge alleged that the *Jura* had not been scheduled to call at Scutari at all but was bound straight for England, and that this was a doctors' plot to get her out of the way. She and her oddly assorted retinue had a rough passage to Scutari and Florence was again horribly seasick. She was still so weak that she could not feed herself or speak above a whisper, her hair had been cropped during the fever, she was pale and emaciated – a changed woman. She was never fully to recover her physical strength again.

Weak as she was, she would not listen to the doctors who urged her to return to England. 'If I go, all this will go to pieces,' she wrote. The

OPPOSITE Lord Raglan (left) consulting with Omar Pasha (centre) and General Pélissier (right), photographed by Fenton. At the time of the Crimean War he had not seen active service for nearly forty years, and it was rumoured that he had a habit of referring to the enemy as 'the French'.

Parthenope's idealized sketch of Lord Raglan visting Florence during her illness. He was to die shortly afterwards.

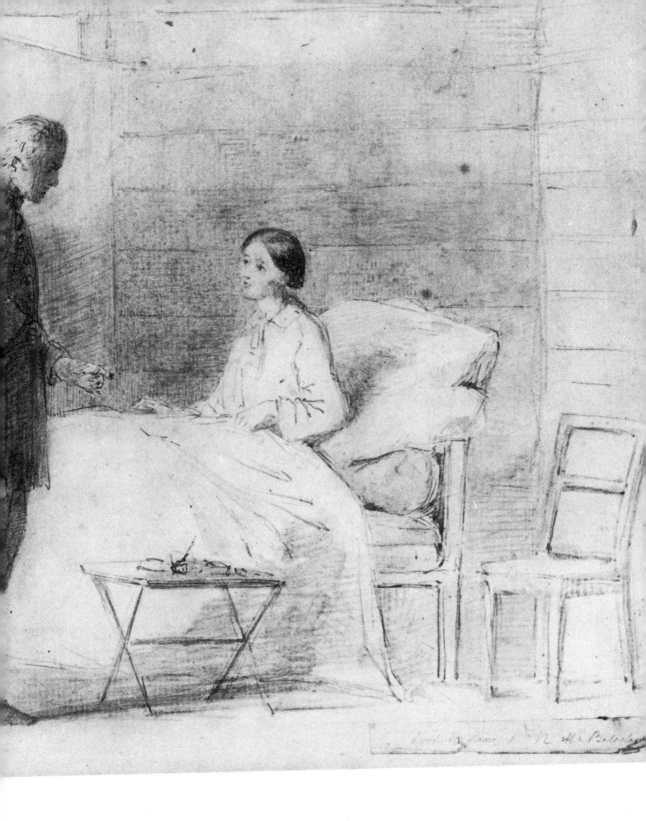

chaplain's house was put at her disposal, and in July she recovered with surprising speed. But on the 28th the Bracebridges left her. They had been invaluable, coping with so many of the day-to-day tasks such as the running of the Free Gifts Store for which Selina had made herself responsible, but they were worn out and their health was suffering. It was a great blow to Florence – 'no one can tell what she has been to me,' she wrote of Selina – but she did not attempt to dissuade them. When they left Scutari, Florence returned to the Barrack Hospital and resumed her duties there.

The crisis of the hospitals was past, but new ones had arisen. Scutari was now full of convalescents who had nothing to do and nothing on which to spend their pay but drink. And drink they did, rot-gutting spirits brewed by Turks and Greeks which caused the soldiers to be carried back to their quarters '*dead* drunk (for they die of it), and officers look on with composure and say to me, "You are spoiling the brutes"'. The real horrors of war, Florence had written to her mother, were not wounds and blood and fevers but 'intoxication, drunken brutality, demoralization, and disorder on the part of the inferior; jealousies, meanness, indifference, selfish brutality on the part of the superior'.

It was not her nature to stand by and see men she had nursed through wounds and sickness – increasingly she thought of them as 'my children' – destroyed by idleness and drink. Before her visit to the Crimea, she had opened a small reading-room within the Barrack Hospital. So popular did it prove that she asked permission to engage a schoolmaster to instruct the illiterate, but this was going too far in the direction of spoiling the brutes, and Lord William Paulet refused. However, he could not stop her from devoting one afternoon a week to receiving from the men money they wished to remit to their families, for which the army had no satisfactory system. Soon £1,000 a month was coming in, which she sent to her uncle Sam Smith, who bought and distributed postal orders.

Facilities to read and save did not eliminate drunkenness, but they sensibly reduced it. In September 1855 Lord William Paulet was replaced by General Henry Storks, who proved far more helpful. He took over a building, equipped it for recreation – the Inkerman Café – and had two teachers sent out. Through the Nightingale Fund established in England as a mark of thanksgiving for Florence's recovery, equipment arrived by the crateload. 'How hard we worked to send off boxes for F's education of the army!' Parthe wrote. 'We have sent a dose of a thousand copybooks, writing materials in proportion, diagrams, maps, *Macbeth* to read six at a time . . . chess, footballs, other games, a magic lantern for dissolving views, a stereoscope (very fine!), plays for acting, music etc.' The Queen contributed a print of the Duke of Wellington presenting flowers to his godson, Prince Arthur. She also sent Florence a brooch designed by Prince Albert as her personal 'mark of esteem and gratitude for her devotion towards the Queen's brave soldiers'. Florence was not one to miss an opportunity to enlist the Sovereign's aid. In her letter of thanks, she outlined the causes of army drunkenness and its remedies. The Queen sent her letter on to the Cabinet. The Prime Minister, Palmerston, called it excellent but Lord Panmure thought it only went to show how little Florence knew of the British soldier, who, he wrote to Lord Raglan's successor, 'is not a remitting animal'.

He was wrong. Over £71,000 was sent home in the next six months: all of it money, as Florence said, saved from the drink-shops. Once again it was her personal influence over the men that made her plans succeed. Once again she was everywhere – drawing up the price-list for the Inkerman Café, providing writing-paper, arranging the men's personal affairs. In January 1856 she wrote to a chaplain in Kent that she had 'just seen Thomas Whybron, 12th Lancers, and that he has promised me that he will not only write to his wife, but transmit money to her through me after 1st of next month. . . . She had better also write to him herself, and send her letter through me. . . . He is well, but has been in debt.' Trooper Whybron was far from being the only soldier whose personal affairs she straightened out. In knowledge of the common soldier, she could leave Lord Panmure at the post.

Not only did the men send money home to their wives but they crowded into lectures, attended singing classes and even got up amateur theatricals. Florence observed that their writing-room was as orderly and silent as the library of the British Museum. It was virtually her personal discovery that, despite the fixed contrary belief of most officers and

authorities, the 'brutal and licentious soldiery' were brutalized by circumstances and not by nature, and that decent treatment could arouse a decent response. Perhaps her greatest achievement in the Crimea was to change the image of the British soldier from that of a man apart, brave in battle but in barracks coarse, drunken and fit only to be disciplined by the whip, into that of a fellow-citizen with the same needs, hopes, feelings and fears as the ordinary mortal. 'She taught officers and officials,' a sympathizer wrote, 'to treat the soldiers as Christian men.' Although they were not always so treated in later years, an irreversible change had taken place in the public attitude towards the army; and the two individuals who did most to bring this about were Florence, the first of the women nurses, and William Russell, the first of the war correspondents in the modern style.

When she returned to the Barrack Hospital in August 1855, Florence had been nine months on active service, and the heroic days were over. She had still a year to serve and the hardest struggles lay ahead: hardest because they were concerned with personalities, pettiness and in-fighting, rather than the life and death of stricken men.

In London, a packed and wildly enthusiastic public meeting, held on 29 November 1855, chaired by the Duke of Cambridge and addressed by Sidney Herbert, the Duke of Argyll, Lord Lansdowne, Monckton Milnes and other notables, launched the Nightingale Fund to mark the nation's veneration for its new saint – she was freely likened to Joan of Arc – and its gratitude for her recovery. Subscriptions poured in; the voluntary contribution of one day's pay brought in £9,000 from the army in the Crimea. Dr Hall and certain other senior officers refused to subscribe.

To some extent, Florence brought this hostility on herself. Compromise, give and take, flattery, equivocation, she despised. What she believed to be right, that she would do. While always correct in her outward deference to military discipline, she could be arrogant and self-righteous. 'They [the soldiers] are much more respectful to me than they are to their own officers,' she wrote: a fact hardly likely to endear her to the officers. To blame came more naturally to her than to praise, and she had been free with her blame. She herself was under no illusions. 'There

OPPOSITE (LEFT) A bracelet presented to Florence in 1855 by the Sultan of Turkey.

(RIGHT) A gold and diamond brooch presented to Florence by Queen Victoria. It was designed by Prince Albert.

is not an official,' she wrote, 'who would not burn me like Joan of Arc if he could, but they know that the War Office cannot turn me out because the country is with me.' She added: 'The real grievance against us is that, though subordinate to the Medical Chiefs in Office, we are superior to them in influence and in the chance of being heard at home.'

Herself always careful to work this influence behind the scenes, she was furious when Charles Bracebridge publicly attacked the army medical authorities in a lecture in Coventry in October 1855, full of exaggerations and mistakes – 'twaddling nonsense' according to Dr Andrew Smith. She wrote scathingly to her old friend that his remarks justified all the attacks made against her and that they were 'utterly unfair'. She was still a sick woman, and the note of self-pity and near-hysteria that appears in many of her writings at this time was sounded in a letter to her aunt Mai written on 5 November 1855, the anniversary of her arrival at Scutari:

What a twelvemonth of dirt it has been, of experience which would sadden not a life but eternity. Who has ever had a sadder experience. Christ was betrayed by one, but my cause has been betrayed by everyone – ruined, destroyed, betrayed by everyone alas one may truly say excepting Mrs Roberts, Rev Mother and Mrs Stewart [Miss Shaw Stewart]. . . . And Mrs Stewart is more than half mad. A cause which is supported by a mad woman and twenty fools must be a falling house.

Dr Hall, she added, 'descends to every meanness', and she accused him of 'attempting to root me out of the Crimea'.

The fall of Sebastopol on 8 September 1855 neither ended the war nor emptied the hospitals. On 9 October she returned to the Crimea. Her position, like her health, had deteriorated. Raglan had gone, some of her best nurses had died, others had married and Dr Hall was openly ignoring her authority. Without consulting her, he had arranged the transfer of thirteen Irish Roman Catholic nuns under the Reverend Mother Bridgeman from the Koulali Hospital to the General Hospital at Balaclava. This was not only a personal affront but a challenge to all she had been trying to achieve. In addition, the 'extra-diet' kitchens planned with M Soyer had not been built, and when she sent a cook to Balaclava at her own expense, he had been refused employment.

In the Crimea, where an acute attack of sciatica forced her into the Castle Hospital again, her main task was to deal with the Reverend Mother Bridgeman, whose defiance was not just a matter of pride or pique. It was a matter, in Florence's view, of the success or failure of the whole experiment of introducing women nurses into military hospitals. Unless the nurses formed a unified, disciplined body under a recognized commander like any other military unit, the whole project would disintegrate. Dr Hall had never admitted this, nor acknowledged her authority – she thought he wanted the project to disintegrate. 'He does not think it beneath his dignity to broil me slowly upon the fire of my own extra-diet kitchen,' she wrote. He had fallen out with Miss Shaw-Stewart over the matter of making toast for officers, reprimanded her orderlies over her head and accused her nursing staff of insubordination – unlike Mother Bridgeman's far more obliging nuns at the General Hospital. 'Mother Brickbat's conduct', Florence wrote, 'has been neither that of a Christian, a gentlewoman, or even a woman.' Mother Brickbat got on well with Dr Hall.

Before she could resolve the situation, Florence was summoned back to Scutari to cope with another outbreak of cholera in November 1855. Once again the wards were full; once again soldiers, nurses and surgeons were dying. Among the first to go was Dr McGrigor.

When the Bracebridges had returned to England, Florence's aunt Mai had volunteered to fill Selina's place. It was a heroic decision. Aunt Mai was a gentle, not a forceful, character; shy not sophisticated; impulsive, affectionate, unselfish and utterly devoted to her niece. The discomforts, crudities and intrigues of Scutari were something wholly alien to her sheltered life, and when she saw the changes they had wrought in Florence, now pale and emaciated with hair cut short like a child's, she burst into tears. The pressure of administrative work had forced Florence virtually to give up nursing, the work she loved; a daily walk round the wards with Mrs Roberts was her only recreation; 'seeing a stream of people and writing is her life'.

Suppose you could see us just now at 12.30 by the little black clock just about to strike its half-hour, you would see us back to back, Flo at her large table covered with papers, I at my little table with my tiny work. We speak not a

OVERLEAF An attack on the Malakoff fort, before the final capitulation of the Russians at Sebastopol. A lithograph by Simpson.

Christmas dinner on the
heights before Sebastopol.
Soldiers of the British army,
though far from home,
were able to celebrate the
festival in some style. The
lithograph is by Simpson.

word. The wind roars, the rain patters; I don't think Flo is conscious of the bluster, I never saw a mind so continuously concentrated on her work. Is it a mind that belonged to some other planet? . . . For it does not seem adapted to the human frame, though it has forced that frame to obedience.

The frame was fragile, the force seemed superhuman at times.

She continually writes till one or two, sometimes till three or four; has in the last pressure given up three whole nights to it. We seldom get through even our little dinner (after it has been put off one, two, or even three hours on account of her visitors) without her being called away from it. I never saw a greater picture of exhaustion than Flo last night at ten (7 Jan). 'Oh, do go to bed,' I said. 'How can I; I have all those letters to write,' pointing to the divan covered with papers. 'Write them tomorrow.' 'Tomorrow will bring its own work.' And she sat up the greater part of the night.

Sat up in cold and discomfort; she had no fire, because the stove smoked; icy draughts swept through the ill-fitting windows. And yet, 'She has attained a most wonderful calm and presence of mind. She is, I think, often deeply impressed, and depressed, though she does not show it outwardly, but no irritation of temper, no hurry or confusion of manner, ever appears for a moment.' And despite everything, 'we laugh at times over these circumstances and she still looks blooming in the face.' She even retained an interest in clothes: 'Flo was delighted with her gloves, and much rejoiced to hear of slippers.'

I am sure she is low in bonnets, only take care, please, if you send one, that it is in the plain style which alone she will wear. She is always handsomely and nicely dressed, but perfectly plain, a black gown and black shawl when she goes out. In the house she never wears any shawl or cloak; she can't bear to have her arms at all embarrassed.

A good deal of all this toil was not only distasteful but unnecessary, brought about by petty spite and jealousy. There was a prolonged and time-wasting affair concerning a Miss Salisbury who had been caught red-handed stealing large quantities of stores, and dismissed; back in London, she spread calumnies on which Florence's enemies in the War Office seized, forcing a semi-official enquiry. Florence had to spend hour after weary hour writing a detailed report to refute Miss Salisbury's blatant lies. She completed it on Christmas morning – twenty-eight

A rare photograph of Florence taken on her return from the Crimea. Though greatly weakened by her illness, she refused to accept her friends' advice to rest, and pressed on relentlessly with her plans to reform the army medical services.

foolscap pages. Mary Stanley took Miss Salisbury's part and wrote a rambling, incoherent letter mainly about her own spiritual conflict, adding: 'I would work under you if I could, but I do not understand your system. . . . God bless you, my dearest friend, and give me one line to say you still love me.' Florence's reply was brutal: 'I have no Mary Stanley, and to her who I once thought my Mary Stanley I have nothing to write. She has injured my work.' Their friendship was never mended.

At least she had a brief let-up that Christmas Day (1855), when she attended a party given by the Stratfords. One of her fellow-guests thought she was a nun, from her black dress and close cap.

I felt quite numb as I looked at her wasted figure and the short brown hair combed over her forehead like a child's. . . . She is very slight, rather above the middle height; her face is long and thin. . . . She has a very prominent nose, slightly Roman; and small dark eyes, kind, yet penetrating; but her face does not give you at all the idea of great talent. She looks a quiet, persevering, orderly, lady-like woman.

Still too weak to join in the games, she sat on a sofa and watched, laughing till the tears came into her eyes.

As if Miss Salisbury's calumnies were not enough, the Chief Purveyor in the Crimea, Mr David Fitzgerald, had compiled a report which Dr Hall sent to the War Office, accusing the nurses of insubordination, drunkenness, immorality and extravagance, and disputing Florence's claim to be their Superintendent. The only nurses he commended were Mother Bridgeman's nuns. This report was treated in an extraordinary way. It was shown by a War Office official to Lady Cranworth, who passed on its substance, but Florence herself never set eyes on it. Yet she was advised to reply. So she faced another bout of writing to refute accusations she had never actually seen. These were, she said, a tissue of malicious lies and she was able to prove it.

But help was at hand. The final report by Sir John McNeill and Colonel Tulloch published in January 1856 confirmed all that she had told Sidney Herbert and others about the state of affairs in the medical branch of the army. And Lord Panmure had not swallowed whole the anti-Nightingale views of his permanent officials. In October 1855 he had sent Colonel John Lefroy to the Crimea as a kind of spy, to report to him direct about the state of the hospitals and the truth behind all these accusations and quarrels. Colonel Lefroy sized up the situation and came down unequivocally on Florence's side. Jealousy among the senior medicos was at the bottom of the trouble. 'They would gladly upset her position tomorrow.' He recommended that 'A General Order, recognizing and defining her position, would save her much annoyance and harassing correspondence. It is due, I think, to all she has done and sacrificed.' This, at last, was all that she had hoped for. 'I am fighting for the very existence of our work,' she had written on 20 February 1856 to Sidney Herbert. 'I desire for the sake of that work that it should be placed in General Orders.' 'May I ask you, dear Mr Herbert, to crown your enduring kindness to me by, if you see it desirable, conferring with Col Lefroy in this matter and urging upon the War Department to telegraph my powers to the Military and Medical Authorities in the Crimea and to myself? The Hospitals wait.'

Despite spirited opposition within the War Office, on 16 March 1856 the following statement from the Secretary of State for War was included in the day's General Orders:

It appears to me that the Medical Authorities of the Army do not correctly comprehend Miss Nightingale's position as it has been officially recognized by me. I therefore think it right to state to you briefly for their guidance, as well as for the information of the Army, what the position of that excellent lady is. Miss Nightingale is recognized by Her Majesty's Government as the General Superintendent of the Female Nursing Establishment of the military hospitals of the Army. No lady, or sister, or nurse, is to be transferred from one hospital to another, or introduced into any hospital, without consultation with her. Her instructions, however, require to have the approval of the Principal Medical Officer in the exercise of the responsibility thus vested in her. The Principal Medical Officer will communicate with Miss Nightingale upon all subjects connected with the Female Nursing Establishment, and will give his directions through that lady.

Here at last was victory, affirmation of all that she had worked for, and triumph over Dr Hall. It came a year too late. A year of stupid, vexatious and exhausting struggle eaten by the locusts; the struggle was won, and so was the war. Peace was signed in Paris a fortnight later.

Nevertheless the work of the hospitals was not over. On 24 March Florence landed again at Balaclava, in a blizzard. She had come mainly to instal ten nurses at a hospital recently opened for the Land Transport Corps. She also wished to reconcile her differences with Mother Bridgeman, whom she hoped to conciliate, not to reprimand. When Mother Bridgeman refused, in her own words, 'to connect myself and my Sisters with her', Florence asked her to think it over for a week. All in vain. Mother Bridgeman and her nuns resigned in a body and on 11 April 1856 sailed for home.

Florence, summoning three more of her team from Scutari, had to take over at the General Hospital. She found the nurses' quarters locked, and was told that Mr Fitzgerald had the keys. She sent a message asking for them, and saying she would wait outside until they came. It was snowing, blowing and bitterly cold. She was exhausted by a day, one of many, spent largely on horseback, riding about between the various hospitals five or six miles apart. 'I have never been off my horse until nine or ten at night,' she wrote to Sidney Herbert, 'except when it was too dark to ride home over those crags even with a lantern, when I have gone on foot. During the greater part of the day I have been without food necessarily, except a little brandy and water (you see I am taking to drink like my comrades of the Army).' Yet still she had to wait in the snow hour after hour for the keys of the nurses' quarters. Only after nightfall did they come.

The state of the General Hospital shocked her and her Bermondsey nuns. The patients were dirty and verminous, their bedsores in some cases appalling. It took them two days to clean the building and three days to clean the patients and put the hospital on a proper footing, with Mrs Roberts in charge. Florence slew a rat on the rafters above a patient's bed with one blow of her parasol. Then there was the Land Transport Hospital to attend to which was full of men suffering for exactly the same causes that had all but destroyed the army the year before: exposure, inadequate rations badly cooked, insanitary camps, frostbite and the rest. It seemed that in a year nothing had been learned, nothing amended. In a long letter to Sidney Herbert, written after 10 p.m. 'on my return to my hut upon a pitch-dark, snowy night, after having been fifteen hours on foot or on horseback, and always without food', she gave way to an outburst of despair: 'Believe me when I say that everything in the Army (in point of routine *versus* system) is just where it was eighteen months ago. The only difference is that we are now rolling in stores. But indeed so we were then, but most of them were at Varna. *Nous n'avons rien oublié ni rien appris* [We have forgotten nothing and learned nothing].' What especially embittered her was the treatment of those most responsible, in her view, for the Crimean tragedy. Instead of being sacked with ignominy, Mr Fitzgerald had just been promoted, and Dr Hall awarded the KCB. 'We know what filled the Crimean graves last winter. KCB I believe now means Knight of the Crimean Burying Grounds.'

In some ways these last three and a half months in the Crimea were the bitterest part of her experience. Despite the clarification of her position, she felt the hand of authority against her at every turn. Among the staunchest of her allies was M Soyer, concocting from army rations ever more appetizing menus, which he had framed in parchment and hung in every kitchen; training soldier-cooks, and building extra-diet kitchens for Miss Nightingale. After she had been upset out of an open mule-cart, an officer gave her a hooded baggage-cart, and for the rest of her time in the Crimea she used this as her means of transport. Following her departure, M Soyer, considering it 'a precious relic for present and future generations', rescued it from some Tartar Jews who were about to sell it for scrap and had it shipped to England at his own expense; it is to be seen today at St Thomas' Hospital.

Like the soldiers, the nurses were going home. Among the first to go, after a serious illness at Scutari, was the Reverend Mother of the Bermondsey nuns, whom Florence loved above all her colleagues. 'What you have done for the work, no one can ever say,' she wrote. 'My love and gratitude will be yours, dearest Reverend Mother, wherever you go.' Miss Shaw-Stewart, who despite being 'half mad' had kept the Castle Hospital on its feet from first to last, left the Crimea. 'Without her,' Florence wrote, 'our Crimean work would have come to grief – without her judgment, her devotion, her unselfish, consistent looking to the one great end... her accuracy in all trusts and accounts, her truth, her faithfulness.'

Florence riding in the
hooded army baggage-cart
presented to her by an
officer after she was thrown
from a mule-cart.

The professional nurses could not 'be thrown off like an old shoe'. Their work had been admirable, their manners and morals less so. Florence summed up each individual. One was 'hard-working in Cholera and Fever – one fault, intemperance'. Another was 'kind, clever, useful, good nurse, but deteriorating both as to sobriety and propriety, the latter more to be deplored as she is a married woman'. One was 'too much of a fine lady to be a good nurse (fonder of sketching than of poulticing)'. Another had been 'sent home in disgrace on account of clandestine meetings and reckless falsehood'. To some Florence gave money to tide them over when they got home. She secured a free passage for a buffalo calf that Jane Evans, the former farm-worker, had reared.

Early in July she returned to Scutari, and the last patient left the Barrack Hospital on 16 July 1856. Now came the time for praises. Florence praised her nurses, Panmure praised her in a flowery despatch and General Storks wrote that of all the tributes, he knew she would value most 'the grateful recognition of the poor men you came to succour and to save. You will ever live in their remembrance, be assured of that; for among the faults and vices which ignorance has produced, and a bad system has fostered and matured, ingratitude is not one of the defects of the British soldier.' She knew that; and now that it was all over, she was haunted by thoughts of those she had not been able to save. 'Oh my poor men,' she wrote in one of the notes she still scribbled in times of stress. 'I am a bad mother to come home and leave you in your Crimean graves – seventy-three per cent in eight regiments in six months from disease alone – who thinks of that now?' Florence thought of it for the rest of her life.

Declining the offer of a passage in a man-of-war, she and Aunt Mai embarked on 28 July 1856, travelling incognito as Mrs and Miss Smith. A heroine's welcome awaited her. Military bands, triumphal arches, mayoral addresses, probably Freedoms of Cities, these were being planned. Her dread of public appearance and laurel leaves was almost pathological. She managed to slip undetected into England, where she 'lay lost for a night in London', in the words of Sir Edward Cook. At eight o'clock next morning she rang the bell of the convent of the Bermondsey nuns, who were in retreat, and prayed with them for a few hours. Then she caught a train for Derbyshire, walked from the station to Lea Hurst and, on 7 August 1856, took her family by surprise. Next morning a peal on the village church bells and a prayer of thanksgiving were, her sister wrote, 'all the innocent greeting' – except that provided by what Parthe called the 'spoils of war' who had preceded her: a one-legged sailor boy, a small Russian orphan and a large puppy found in some rocks near Balaclava. England was ringing with her name, but she had left her heart on the battlefields of the Crimea and in the graveyards of Scutari.

The Health of
the Army

CHAPTER SIX

THE HEALTH OF THE ARMY

'THE DIAMOND HAS SHOWN ITSELF,' wrote Sidney Herbert, 'and it must not be allowed to return to the mine.' It had no intention of so doing. There was work to be done, a pledge to be redeemed. 'I stand at the altar of the murdered men and while I live I shall fight their cause,' she wrote. Those men had been murdered by a system – a system deeply entrenched, immensely powerful, hallowed by tradition and essentially masculine. It was this system she now set herself to change.

PREVIOUS PAGES The Coalition Ministry the year of the outbreak of the Crimean War, painted by John Gilbert in 1855. In the front row, from left to right, are Sir James Graham, Gladstone, the Marquis of Lansdowne, Aberdeen, Palmerston and the Duke of Newcastle. Behind them, from left to right, are Sir Charles Wood, Sir William Molesworth, the Duke of Argyll, the Earl of Clarendon, Lord Russell, the Earl of Granville, Lord Cranworth, Sir George Grey and Sidney Herbert.

Within a day or two of her arrival at Lea Hurst, ill and emaciated as she was, nauseated by the sight of food, she wrote to Lord Panmure and to Sidney Herbert asking for interviews. It was August. Panmure was in Scotland shooting grouse, Herbert in Ireland catching salmon. Panmure replied that she must surely be in need of rest, Herbert passed on the advice of his Carlsbad doctor: '*Ni lire, ni écrire, ni réflechir* [Don't read, write or think]'. No advice could have been more unacceptable. Florence did all three with unremitting industry, and Sidney Herbert wrote expressing concern about her overwrought state of mind.

Invitations poured in entreating her to address meetings, accept tributes, attend functions; she refused them all. The showiness, 'fuz-buz about my name', she despised. She was 'as merry about little things as ever', Parthe wrote, but in private notes she poured out her frustrations, and to Colonel Lefroy, now back at the War Office, she wrote of the 'detestation with which I am regarded by the officials'. Her chief enemy was Sir

Benjamin Hawes, Permanent Under-Secretary at the War Office and an implacable opponent of reform.

Then, quite unexpectedly, came an opportunity to state her case at the highest level of all. The Queen wanted to hear of her experiences at first hand. The royal physician, Sir James Clark, invited Florence to stay at his Scottish home near Balmoral. She set to work with enormous thoroughness to prepare her case. Sir John McNeill lived in Edinburgh and she arranged to stay with him *en route*, and summoned thither Colonel Tulloch.

One of the reasons for Florence's success was that she knew exactly what she wanted to achieve. She never waffled. She wanted the root-and-branch reform of the army medical services and knew that the way to go about it, for a start, was to have a Royal Commission. Both its composition and the gist of its recommendations were already clear in her mind. Four days were spent in Edinburgh in conclave with McNeill and Tulloch. Florence was still weak, food still nauseated her, but she spent what little free time she had inspecting barracks and hospitals. On 15 September 1856 she arrived at Sir James Clark's home, Birk Hall, and two days later her first interview with the Queen and the Prince Consort took place.

It was a crucial interview, and a complete success. Florence was a woman after the Queen's own heart. Prince Albert's, too. 'She put before us all the defects of our present military hospital system, and the reforms that are needed. We are much pleased with her; she is extremely modest.' A few days later the Queen drove over to Birk Hall and they had 'tea and a great talk'. Other visits followed; she had conquered the Queen, who wrote to her cousin the Duke of Cambridge, the Commander-in-Chief: 'I wish we had her at the War Office.' No wonder Florence's 'hopes were somewhat raised'. But only somewhat; she knew quite well the limits of the royal powers. Lord Panmure was the man who really mattered. Panmure was due to pay a visit to Balmoral, and the Queen thought it would help Florence's cause if she were to meet the Minister under the royal roof. 'I don't,' Florence wrote bluntly, 'but I am obliged to succumb.' The Queen attempted a little softening up in advance. 'Lord Panmure', she wrote, 'will be much gratified and

Sir James Clark, the
Queen's physician: a
contemporary engraving.
He used his influence to help
Florence to win acceptance
for her plans for army
reform, and sat on the
subcommittee of the
Nightingale Fund Council
for the foundation of a
nursing school at St
Thomas'.

struck with Miss Nightingale – her powerful, clear head, and simple, modest manner.' But Sidney Herbert was 'not sanguine: for, tho' he [Panmure] has plenty of shrewd sense, there is a *vis inertiae* in his hesitance which is very difficult to overcome'.

Panmure was a past master in the art of ignoring or avoiding trouble. Anything in the nature of what we now call a confrontation was anathema, and work, Herbert wrote, 'he found easy through the simple process of never attempting to do it.' He had been angry with McNeill and Tulloch for writing such a harmful report, and did his best to smother it. A Royal Commission that would stir up even murkier waters was clearly the last thing to be desired. He was altogether a much tougher proposition than the Queen.

Widely experienced as he was in resisting pressure, knowing as he did that Florence's iron will and relentless perseverance would be sure to create trouble, he allowed himself to be beguiled. 'You fairly overcame Pan,' Sir James Clark's son wrote to her. 'We found him with his mane absolutely silky, and a loving sadness pervading his whole being.' Sidney Herbert wrote that 'he was very much surprised at your physical appearance, as I think you must have been with his.' Panmure had probably expected a hatchet-faced amazon, instead of this demure, frail, soft-spoken, modest lady – everyone stressed her modesty. By the end of their talks, she had won every point. There was to be a Royal Commission; she was to be invited to submit a full report with her recommendations; her proposal that an Army Medical School should be set up was well received; and finally 'the Bison', on his own initiative, offered to submit to her the plans of the first General Military Hospital to be built in Britain, at Netley, for her comments. It seemed to be a total victory.

Now she set to work in earnest, in consultation with McNeill, Tulloch and Lefroy, Dr Sutherland and others of the 'Crimean confederates', as they became known. The first step was to get the right men for the Commission. The chairmanship was vital. Only one man, of course, could do the job and that was Sidney Herbert. He had been overworking, he was tired, his health was poor and he did not come at once to London to see her. But she was not to be denied. On 16 November 1856 he

called on her at the Burlington Hotel and agreed to accept the chairmanship if it were offered to him. Florence saw that it was.

Then there was the question of the other members. She wanted Dr
Thomas Alexander, who had served with distinction in the Crimea as
surgeon to the Light Division – a 'gentle giant of a Scotchman', in
Russell's words. His independence and out-spokenness had won him a
second-class appointment in Canada, well out of the way. Now
Florence wanted him back. 'The Bison' refused. They agreed about most
other names. 'Seeing him in such a coming-on disposition,' she wrote to
Herbert, 'I was so good as to leave him Dr Smith the more so I could not
help it.' She took the opportunity to score another point. Dr (later Sir)
Andrew Smith would shortly be retiring and the obvious choice as his
successor was Sir John Hall. Florence knew that if he were appointed,
he would sabotage the reforms the Commission was designed to recommend. So she managed to make 'the Bison' promise that he would not
give the job to Hall. There was nothing in this of personal spite, any
more than of pity. Hall was an anti-reformer and Hall must go. He did
not get another job, but lived abroad for the sake of economy and died
ten years later, a disappointed man.

To Sidney Herbert she wrote: 'You must drag it through. If not you,
no one else.' On 22 November 1856 Herbert accepted the chairmanship
in a curiously half-hearted letter to Panmure. 'I am not without doubt
as to the advisability of a Commission'; there was a 'strong professional
feeling in the Army Medical Department which is averse to all change'.
Reform might have a better prospect if it could be brought about from
within. However, since a Commission there must be, he would accept
the office. He made Alexander's appointment a condition of his own.
To this he got no official answer. 'The Bison' had retreated into a convenient patch of cover and sent a 'short note of a friendly character', in
reply, regretting that he was unable to write officially as he had gout in
both hands. 'Gout is a very handy thing,' commented Florence.

The Hawes party in the War Office were hard at work on 'the Bison'.
Florence raged at the delay, but took comfort from her discovery that
'the Bison is always bullyable, remember that'. Sidney Herbert was
incited to do the bullying. On 12 February 1857 he wrote to Panmure:

OPPOSITE Queen Victoria
awards decorations to
wounded officers and
soldiers from the Crimea in
May 1856. This drawing
appeared in an issue of *The
Illustrated London News* in
June 1887, the year of
Victoria's first Jubilee.

'I trust you have sent for Alexander. If you have not, pray do so without loss of time. . . . Will you let me know whether you have sent for Alexander, or whether you can do so by the first available post?' To this there was no reply.

Florence was in despair. Like the Cheshire cat, the Royal Commission was fading away to leave the kind of grin that skeletons display. All the misery and horror of the Crimea seemed to have been forgotten. The real tragedy of the Crimean catastrophe, she wrote, began when it was over. She had one more weapon in her armoury, and this she prepared to use.

The Lady with a Lamp had become a national legend. And this legend she had done her best to destroy. She could not, in fact, destroy it, but she could bury it and trust that time would do the rest. Never once, after her return from Scutari, did she make a public appearance, issue a public statement or write or speak in public about her experiences. From the public's point of view, she simply vanished. But she knew quite well that were she to reappear, the public would rally to her side. And she knew that this would cause a great deal more embarrassment among the anti-reformers than yielding behind the scenes to pressures they might hope to control. At the end of February 1857 she played her last card.

'Three months from this day I publish my experiences of the Crimean campaign, and my suggestions for improvement, unless there has been a fair and tangible pledge by that time for reform.' She had 'the Bison' in a corner now. He had been having a very tiresome winter. Early in the year the two reports by McNeill and Tulloch on the failures of the Commissariat were laid before Parliament and raised a storm. Unfortunately Panmure had omitted to read them until it was too late; he had then, he informed the Queen, done so 'with a view to strike out inconvenient passages, but he found he could not do so successfully unless he struck out or altered the evidence also', which was too much even for 'the Bison'. So the awkward passages stayed in and laid the blame for the 'excessive mortality' in the army squarely on the failures and muddles of the Commissariat; and of the five high-ranking officers named as primarily responsible, four had been promoted and decorated and only one (Filder, the Commissary-General) removed. Then came the Board of General Officers – the Chelsea Board – which exonerated the accused. McNeill and Tulloch were in disgrace. Colonel Tulloch had been led to expect promotion as his reward. When Sir John McNeill wrote to remind Panmure of this promise in February 1856, a note from a secretary informed him that the Minister 'cannot comply with your request, as His Lordship has already enough on his hands about the Commission without promoting Colonel Tulloch'. Neither Commissioner received even a letter of thanks.

Public opinion began to stir. Panmure maladroitly offered the two men £1,000 each. They rejected it with indignation. Sidney Herbert, urged on by Florence, moved a Humble Address in the House of Commons in March 1856, praying her Majesty to bestow a mark of favour on McNeill and Tulloch. It was accepted without a division and Tulloch got a knighthood, while McNeill was sworn in as a Privy Councillor.

All that was tiresome, and so was the matter of the Netley Military Hospital, whose plans Panmure had promised to send to Florence. He did so, and received in response, one may surmise to his dismay, an immensely thorough, carefully compiled, statistically buttressed dissertation on the design of hospitals, based on researches going back to her youth both at home and in France, Germany, Italy and Switzerland. She presented him, in fact, with the fruits of a lifetime's study. These pointed plainly to the conclusion that the design of Netley Hospital was hopelessly out-of-date. She suggested radical changes. Unfortunately Panmure had omitted to enquire how far the building had progressed when he sent her the plans. He now discovered that contracts had been given out, construction commenced and £70,000 already spent; it was too late to make major changes.

Florence went higher: she stayed with the Palmerstons and put the facts before the Prime Minister. As a result, he wrote to Panmure that 'At Netley all consideration of what would best tend to the comfort and recovery of the patients has been sacrificed to the vanity of the architect, whose sole object has been to make a building which should cut a dash when looked at from Southampton river. . . . Pray therefore stop all progress in the work till the matter can be duly considered.'

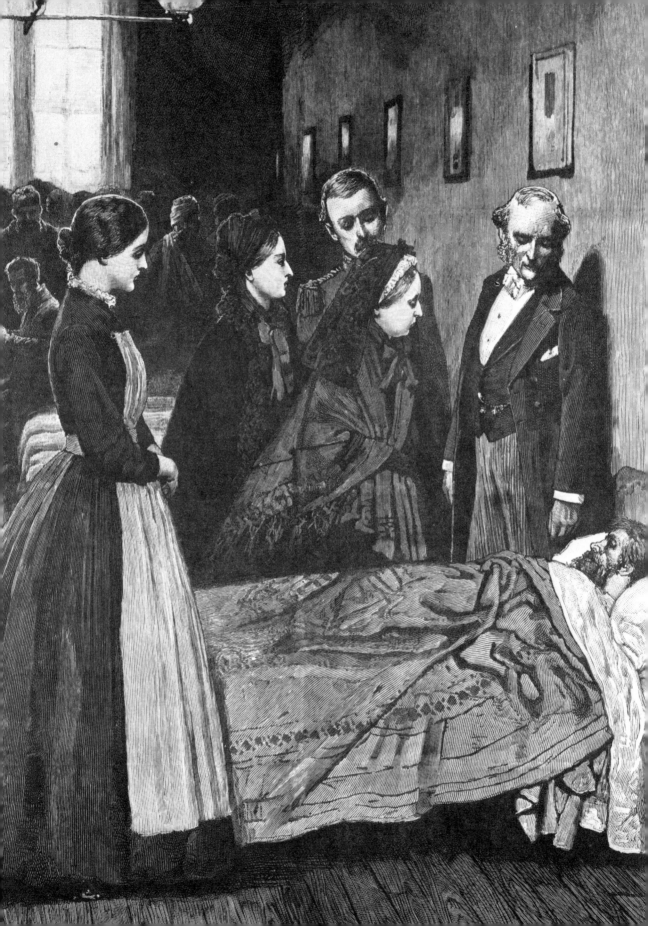

'The Bison' dug in his heels. To justify the waste of £70,000 to Parliament, break contracts and offend everyone concerned seemed likely to cause even more trouble than to disobey his master. In spite of an even stronger letter from Palmerston to say that he would prefer to throw the half-built structure brick by brick into Southampton Water than have a building that was a charnel-house rather than a hospital, Panmure refused to budge. Netley Hospital was completed according to the original plans, although these were modified in detail in ways that Florence suggested.

These experiences convinced 'the Bison' that, beneath the velvet glove of womanly meekness, lay an iron hand of implacable resolve. It would be vain to hope that she would let the Royal Commission on the Sanitary Condition of the Army sink into oblivion. On 27 April 1857 he called on her at the Burlington Hotel and showed her the draft Instructions for the Commission before their submission to the Queen. He also had a list of members, compiled by Dr Andrew Smith. There was a long discussion and she won all her points. 'Every one of the members of the Commission was carried by force of will against Dr Andrew Smith, and poor Pan has been the shuttlecock,' she wrote that evening. 'Pan' was a wily shuttlecock, and before showing the final draft to Dr Smith, took the precaution of getting it initialled by the Queen. What the Queen had approved, the Medical Director-General could not alter. On 5 May the Royal Warrant was signed and the Commission, with Sidney Herbert as chairman, and including Dr Alexander, started work the following week.

Florence now plunged into a vortex of labour. From start to finish this Royal Commission was her child, her creation, and to it she devoted every moment of her time and every atom of her energy. Three months before its appointment, Panmure had invited her to compile a confidential report on her experiences and her views on 'the sanitary requirements of the Army generally'. (Nowadays the word sanitary has come to attach itself mainly to drains; in her day it simply meant health, according to its derivation.) Had Panmure refused the Commission, this would have been the instrument for making good her threat. Now, it was to form the basis of her evidence to the Commission. She refused

OPPOSITE Queen Victoria visting Netley Hospital in May 1863: from *The Illustrated London News* (1887). Here she talks to a dying soldier from India.

to give this in person, but agreed to answer any question submitted to her in writing.

It was a monumental document, heavily laced with statistics, occupying, when privately printed – it was never published – nearly a thousand pages and named *Notes on Matters affecting the Health, Efficiency and Hospital Administration of the British Army.* The basis of her case was simple. Most of the sickness which afflicted the army in peace or war was caused by defects in the system, or lack of system, into whose care the soldier was committed. The Army Medical Services had been formed to treat the sick and wounded when they reached the hospitals; what was needed was a system which would prevent most of the sick ever getting there at all. Given proper food, clothing, shelter, cleanliness and general hygiene, the hospitals would not be filled. Preventative medicine, in other words – so obvious to later generations but then a revolutionary idea. It might be 'spoiling the brutes' to give them 'comforts' but it would also keep them alive.

Statistics hitherto buried in official memoranda were brought into the light of day and produced a tremendous impact. For every man killed in battle or died of wounds in the Crimea, seven had died from diseases, mostly preventable. Even more startling were the facts about the peacetime army. Like all armies, it consisted of young, vigorous men between the ages of seventeen and thirty-five who had passed a medical examination, and who were presumed to be the pick of the nation's manhood. Their rate of mortality should have been far less than the average. In fact, it was double, and often much more than double, that of the population as a whole, including the old, the afflicted, the infants, the women of child-bearing age. In the parish of St Pancras the general mortality was 2·2 per thousand; in the barracks situated therein, that of the Life Guards, it was 10·4 per thousand. In the Borough of Kensington the general rate was 3·3 per thousand; in the Knightsbridge barracks, where the pick of the cavalry was quartered, 17·5 per thousand. These were shocking figures, and she offered no soothing excuses. 'The Army are *picked* lives. . . . Yet the Army . . . dies at twice the rate of mortality of the general population. Fifteen hundred good soldiers are as certainly killed by these neglects yearly as if they were drawn up on Salisbury

Plain and shot.' She added a sentence which caught the public ear: 'Our soldiers enlist to death in the barracks.'

In this massive compendium she had virtually written singlehanded the whole of the Commission's report, and in more forceful English than any official body would use. McNeill read a passage to 'one of the most admired essayists of our time, without telling him what I was reading from. When I had done he said, "That is perfect, whose is that?" I bade him guess. He said, "There are not many men in England who could have done it. It must be some new writer."' McNeill added: 'I regard it as a gift to the Army, and to the country, altogether priceless.'

She was about halfway through this immense task when the Commission began to sit, and was for the next three months in almost daily communication with Sidney Herbert and Dr Sutherland, on whose expert knowledge she drew. These three formed the 'inner cabinet' or steering committee, though one of them was not a member. (Dr Sutherland was.) 'We must meet and agree our course,' Herbert wrote as soon as the Commission began its work. Later, 'I send you Hall's correspondence. You know the matters treated with all the dates which I do not. . . .' 'I should very much like to have a Cabinet Council with you today. Shall I come to you at five o'clock, or would you come here?' She conferred with McNeill on how to handle Dr Hall. There was to be no revenge. 'We do not want to badger the old man in his examination, which would do us no good and him harm. But we want to make the best out of him for our cause. . . .' A note from Liz Herbert read: 'Sidney is again in despair for you, can you come? You will say, *Bless* that man, why can't he leave me in peace? But I am only obeying orders in begging for you.'

At Herbert's request, she coached each witness individually before he gave his evidence, and 'reported to him [Herbert] what each could tell him as a witness in public'. No wonder the Commissioners called her their Commander-in-Chief. 'She is the mainspring of the work,' Dr Sutherland told her aunt Mai. 'Nobody who has not worked with her could know her, could have any idea of her strength and clearness of mind, her extraordinary powers joined with her benevolence of spirit. She is one of the most gifted creatures God ever made.'

Sidney Herbert, the man of whom Florence wrote after his death: 'I loved and served him as no one else,' though she showed little appreciation of his help during his lifetime.

All this she did not only without secretarial help, but in the most cramped, uncomfortable conditions at 'the dingy old Burlington', with one small room opening out of the family sitting-room to work in, and despite the most unhelpful and unfeeling behaviour of her mother and sister. (Her father, more and more ineffectual, had retreated to Embley.) After her triumphal return from Scutari, they were glad enough to bask in her reflected glory. They, too, were at the Burlington, with little to do except go to parties, receive callers, talk about their heroic Flo, sometimes interrupt her work and do nothing to further it. Her only source of income was her father's allowance which was still, in theory, £500 a year, though he must have supplemented it. Fanny insisted on charging Florence for her share of the Burlington bills, and sometimes overcharged her. When the hotel mistakenly let one of the bedrooms in the Nightingale's suite, it was Florence, not Parthe, who had to sleep out in an annex and come in to work and eat.

Fanny and Parthe kept a carriage but Florence had to get about by cab or even omnibus, however inconvenient, and sometimes on foot. Her health was so poor that in the autumn of 1856 Parthe had written 'I cannot believe that she will live long.' Yet in the winter Fanny recorded: 'Yesterday Flo went with Sir John Liddell (Director-General of the Navy Medical Department) and her good angel Hilary to Chatham, setting off at 9½ o'clock and not returning till 9½ at night; thirty miles to Chatham by rail, several miles in cabs and, Sir John said, up to thirty miles walking about the three hospitals.' This was a typical day; in addition to the paper work, she was inspecting hospitals to gather facts and sitting up into the small hours with Dr Sutherland, and often with Dr William Farr, a pioneer in medical statistics, to collate and tabulate them.

The Commission sat throughout the summer of 1857, from May until August. The weather was oppressive, the Season over, yet Fanny and Parthe insisted on staying on to be with Flo, who did not want them. Years later she described to Mary Mohl what she had suffered: 'The whole occupation of Parthe and Mama was to lie on two sofas and tell one another not to get tired by putting flowers into water.' One evening, on her return in a state of exhaustion, Fanny told her, from the sofa, that the Duke of Newcastle had called, adding: 'You lead a very amusing life.' Florence commented bitterly that it was a scene worthy of Molière 'where two people in tolerable and even perfect health, lie on the sofa all day, doing absolutely nothing, and persuade themselves and others that they are the victims of their self-devotion for another who is dying of overwork'.

As she drove herself so she drove others, unmercifully, and in particular the ever-faithful Dr Sutherland. Despite his devotion and ability, he irritated her, and brought out her usually suppressed impatience. Mrs Cecil Woodham-Smith wrote in her biography: 'He met Miss Nightingale at Scutari, became her slave and his career was at an end.' Others have pointed out that, though he ceased to be an Inspector of the Board of Health, his active career continued until he was over eighty and led to influential positions, such as membership of the Royal Commission on India of 1859–63. He put up with a great deal from Florence. Living out at Highgate, sometimes he was late for appointments, or his wife wrote a note asking Florence to excuse him; she reacted sharply. 'My dear lady, do not be unreasonable,' he implored. Once when he had stayed late at the Burlington finishing a report, she sent to Highgate first thing next morning ordering him to return and go through it again. For once he refused, and she got into such a 'half fainting state' that Aunt Mai was despatched to bring him back at any price. He submitted, returned and humbly apologised.

If Florence pressed thus hard on Dr Sutherland, it is easy to imagine the pressure she exerted on Sidney Herbert. Always a hard and quick worker, he was a superb chairman whose 'very manner engaged the most sulky and recalcitrant witnesses', Florence wrote. 'He never made an enemy or a quarrel in the Commission.' The work was completed and the report, with its numerous appendices, written in exactly three months.

Most Blue Books end up in pigeon holes and Florence did not doubt that 'Pan' had a convenient one ready for the Sanitary Commission. Pressure must be applied. On 7 August 1857 Herbert warned him that the report was 'likely to arrest a good deal of general attention' and that he would be wise to start putting its recommendations into effect before its publication. Otherwise he would 'lose the prestige which attaches to rapid action'. Herbert suggested the immediate appointment of four sub-commissions with executive powers and Treasury funds to carry out the main reforms under four heads: improvement of barracks and army hospital buildings; setting up a statistical branch in the Army Medical Department; reconstructing the Director-General's office; and establishing an Army Medical School. Herbert offered to serve himself on any or all of these sub-commissions.

It was August, and Panmure had gone north to shoot grouse. However, Herbert 'caught him on the wing' during a flying visit to London and secured a lukewarm agreement to the sub-commissions. He accepted the chairmanship of all four. His point won, he was 'able to leave for Ireland with a lighter heart' to catch salmon. 'But I am not easy about you,' he wrote to Florence. 'Here am I going to lead an animal life for a month. . . . Why can't you, who do men's work, take man's exercise in some shape?' Dr Sutherland also urged her to take a rest. She refused; but she had reached the end of her tether, and on 11 August she collapsed. Now she craved one thing above all others: solitude. For four years she had never once been alone and it was driving her mad. Rebelling at last against her family, she went to Malvern, taking only a footman. 'It makes us very unhappy to think of her so forlorn and comfortless,' wrote Parthe, still unable to understand.

She was very ill, with a racing pulse, unable to eat solid food and having cold water packs twice a day. 'You must have new blood or you can't work and new blood can't be made out of tea at least so far as I know,' wrote Dr Sutherland. This infuriated her, and she wrote a long rambling reply in which she described a vision of 'my poor owl, without her life, without her talons, lying in the cage of your canary and the little villain pecking at her. Now, that's me. I am lying without my head, without my claws, and you all peck at me.' Sutherland replied soothingly: 'I want you to live, I want you to work. You want to work and die, and that is not at all fair. . . . You little know what daily anxiety it has cost me to see you dying by inches. . . .' Her reply to this was to command him to Malvern on the following Monday to work with her on the sub-commission plans. He found her in a desperate plight.

Her breathing was distressed, she could eat nothing when excited, she could not sleep.

Once more, almost the only close relative who did not reduce Florence to despair was called in – Aunt Mai. By the end of September Florence was well enough, or considered herself to be so, to return, accompanied by her aunt, to the Burlington. Once again she threw herself into the same round of interviews and writing. Parthe announced her intention of returning to her sister's side, Aunt Mai wrote to warn her away; she insisted; Florence had a severe all-night attack of palpitations with pains in the heart and head. Aunt Mai wrote distractedly that 'her life hung by a thread', and that Parthe must at all costs keep away. Parthe stayed at Embley. A further attempt by Fanny and Parthe made in the following spring to join Florence at the Burlington brought on more attacks. They came to London, but stayed at a different hotel. Florence had won one more battle: the last of all the battles with her mother and sister. Perhaps it was their lack of understanding that prompted her to write to Mary Mohl in 1861:

Women have no sympathy. . . . I have never found one woman who has altered her life by one iota for me or my opinions. Now look at my experience of men. A statesman, past middle age, absorbed in politics for a quarter of a century, out of sympathy with me, remodels his whole life and policy – learns a science the driest, the most technical, the most difficult, that of administration, as far as it concerns the lives of men – not, as I learned it, in the field from stirring experience, but by writing dry regulations in a London room by my sofa with me. This is what I call real sympathy. Another (Alexander, whom I made Director-General) does very nearly the same thing. Clough, a born poet if ever there was one, takes to nursing-administration in the same way, for me. But I could mention very many others – Farr, McNeill, Tulloch, Storks, Martin, who in a lesser degree altered their work by my opinions. And, the most wonderful of all, a man born without a soul, like Undine – all these elderly men.

In this last sentence she was grossly unfair to Dr Sutherland, and in the others to her own sex. But the iron of her 'dear people' had bitten deep into her soul.

Meanwhile a strange episode had occurred. In the summer of 1857, when Florence was working herself to death in conclave with Sutherland,

Miss Florence Nightingale.
at Embley.
December 28th 1857.

Florence at Embley in 1857:
a pencil drawing of her by
G. Scharf. This was one of
the most active and fruitful
periods of her life, but as so
often she reacted with
symptoms of nervous
distress.

Herbert, Farr, Alexander and the rest, a tall, exceedingly handsome, rich, benevolent, charming and altogether remarkable baronet began to pay frequent calls at the Burlington. He was a widower of fifty-six, a Liberal MP, the owner of a large estate in Buckinghamshire where he had built model cottages, founded schools and devoted himself to improving the lot of the rural poor. Now this paragon, Sir Harry Verney, proposed to Florence. It must indeed have startled her. She had no thoughts, and certainly no time, for ideas of love and marriage. Fanny invited him to Embley to console him for his rejection, and he proceeded to transfer his affections to Parthe. In June 1858 Parthe became Lady Verney. '*She* likes it, which is the main thing,' Florence wrote to Lady McNeill. 'He is old and rich, which is a disadvantage. He is active, has a will of his own and four children ready-made, which is an advantage. Unmarried life, at least in our own class, takes everything and gives nothing back to this poor earth.'

Florence had made up her mind that she was about to die. In November 1857 she wrote a long letter to Sidney Herbert starting: 'I hope you will not regret the manner of my death. . . . I am sorry not to stay alive to do the "Nurses". But I can't help it. "Lord, here I am, send me," has always been religion to me. I must be willing to go now as I was to go to the East.' Perhaps God, she wrote, wanted a Sanitary Officer 'for my Crimeas in some other world where they are gone'. She hoped that Herbert would have no chivalrous ideas of what was due to her – 'the only thing that can be "due" to me is what is good for the troops. I thought thus while I was alive. And I am not likely to think otherwise now that I am dead.' She made a will, directing that the money she was due to inherit from her father should be used to build a model barracks. Still bitter against her mother, she wrote 'For every one of my eighteen thousand children, for every one of those poor tiresome Harley Street creatures, I have expended more motherly feeling and action in a week than my mother has expended for me in thirty-seven years.'

Dying she might be: until the breath actually left her body, she would work – 'day after day', Aunt Mai noted 'until she is almost fainting'. Aunt Mai was with her at the Burlington but no one else.

For two years the War Office officials, headed by Sir Benjamin

Sir Harry Verney, who married Parthe but retained a strong affection for her younger sister who had rejected his offer of marriage. He was a philanthropist at heart, practising what he believed on his family estates in Buckinghamshire: he set up schools, drained and reclaimed land and tried to enforce the Poor Law. He had also tended the sick during a cholera outbreak in Aylesbury. His aims and ideals therefore came close to Florence's.

Arthur Hugh Clough: a portrait in chalk by S. Rowse. He gave Florence valuable help with her manuscripts. A civil servant working at the Education Office, he was also a talented poet. Some of his poems reflect the religious doubts which caused him to resign two university posts. His death was commemorated in a poem by Matthew Arnold, 'Thyrsis'.

Hawes, fought with skill and pertinacity against the sub-commissions and against their proposed reforms. The Burlington became known as the Little War Office. Day after day people came and went with papers, conferences were held, drafts written and amended, with Florence at the centre and all the threads in her frail-appearing hands.

The time had come to bring into use the vast repository of facts assembled in her still unpublished *Notes on the British Army*. She prepared a summary entitled *Mortality in the British Army*, and had it illustrated by coloured circles, squares and wedges, a technique in which she was a pioneer. Then two thousand copies were printed and she sent a copy, nearly always with a personal letter, to everyone of influence, starting with the Queen. (She called it *Coxcombs*.) Next she drew up a list of every magazine and review she thought important, suggested to each editor the name of a suitable contributor, and to the contributors the lines of the article she wished them to write. Only one editor, and one contributor (Lord Derby), refused to play.

Once again her sheer output of words was almost unbelievable. She had no secretarial help beyond what Aunt Mai could afford her. Her cousin's husband Arthur Clough, to whom she became very devoted, came round sometimes when his work at the Education Office was over, to help correct proofs. In the midst of all this Palmerston's Government fell in February 1858, and 'the Bison' disappeared from the political scene, one may surmise thankfully, back to his deer, grouse and salmon. The following November he wrote from the Highlands apologizing for once having called her 'a turbulent fellow' – 'I must have been vilely rude' – and sent her a peace-offering in the shape of a box of grouse.

Herbert was working himself to death trying to get practical reforms carried through. He personally visited almost every barrack in the country, standing for hours in cold and draughty squares and corridors and appalled by what he saw; non-ventilation in some of the barracks recalled the Black Hole of Calcutta. A valuable ally had been made in the shape of Captain (later Sir) Douglas Galton, a brilliant young engineer who married Florence's cousin Marianne, and became an expert on barrack ventilation and design. And Florence called back into action her Crimean ally M Soyer to redesign the kitchens. Within a month of his opening his first model kitchen, at Wellington Barracks, he was dead – 'a great disaster', Florence said.

The longest and most exasperating struggle of all concerned the founding of an Army Medical School. This was to be a vital part of the pattern of reform. It is hard today to understand why the concept of preventive medicine was then regarded by the bulk of the medical profession as a revolutionary, dangerous and unsound idea. But army doctors had been trained as surgeons, not physicians; the germ theory was still unknown; that diseases could spread as a result of bad ventilation, overcrowding and lack of drainage, that diet and clothing were factors in determining health, were cranky, unproved ideas. The Army Medical School was to come into existence to teach all these wildcat theories, and doubtless others no less far-fetched. It must be resisted, and resisted it was.

Throughout 1858 the War Office on the one hand, and the Little War Office on the other, fought a running battle of files, memoranda and minutes. Nothing would have happened if another change of government had not brought back Palmerston who, in June 1859, put Herbert at the head of the War Office. The way of the reformers now seemed clear. Nearly two years before, in 1857, Florence had drawn up the regulations covering the Medical School and, in consultation with Sir James Clark, nominated the professors. One of Herbert's first acts was to appoint them, and the School was brought officially into being before the end of 1859.

The War Office was by no means defeated. It was not until September 1860 that the first students, ten in number, arrived. They found bare walls, no scientific instruments, no laboratories, nothing at all. The requisitions made by the staff had simply been ignored. Sidney Herbert's biographer, Lord Stanmore, explained what had occurred: 'The estimate [for the fittings and instruments] had been sent in by the professors early in April but had not received the sanction of the Treasury until late in August. The "authority to expend" was sent first to the Tower, whence it was returned with the remark that no surgical instruments were kept there. It was next despatched to the arsenal at Woolwich, which could only supply guns.' Weaving its way back to the Director-General at the War Office, whence it had come, it came to rest on the desk of an Assistant Under-Secretary of State where it would have been decently buried had not 'a trenchant letter from Miss Nightingale called back the personal interposition of the Secretary of State'.

Florence's concern was with army health, a subject vast enough in all conscience, but only one of the enormous number with which Herbert had to deal. He had also to take part in Cabinet meetings, to attend the House of Commons – in 1860 he spoke there more than two hundred times – to cope with a war in China, and to lead the full social life of a popular and sociable man. The smallest, most insignificant matters wound their way along the sluggish channels of bureaucracy, gathering minutes like barnacles as they went, until they reached the desk of the Minister himself. To give a single example: a dispute between the Principal Medical Officer of Yarmouth and the Steward of the General Hospital concerning some fowls belonging to the Steward which had strayed into the hospital grounds. The Steward, moreover, had employed an orderly to dig his potatoes. The Steward riposted that the PMO had used a hospital rug as a carpet and washed his dog in a hospital bath. All this, heavily minuted, reached Herbert's desk for his personal adjudication. It was little wonder that his health suffered. Throughout 1858 he was afflicted by neuralgia, acute headaches and pleurisy, and had to drive himself to keep going. From Florence he got scant sympathy. Had not her life been despaired of, and was she not still alive? So long as the Cause needed them, the body must obey the will. And the Cause needed them more than ever. The inefficiency, delays and obstruction had convinced Herbert that he must tackle the enormous task of the root-and-branch reform of the War Office itself. This was to be, in Florence's words, 'one fight more, the best and the last'.

She flung herself into it with her usual almost gruesome energy. 'I am being worked on a treadmill,' she wrote. Her fits of breathlessness, fainting and aversion to food grew worse again and in the late summer of 1859 she moved to Hampstead into furnished rooms. Thither Herbert rode out to see her from his house in Belgrave Square, and consultations went on evening after evening when his work at the War Office was done.

From now on, Florence became a permanent invalid. Weak, frail and emaciated, the least activity was liable to bring on palpitations. She was under forty; she had another fifty years to live; but the rest of her life was spent mainly in her bed or on a sofa. There was generally a cat or two on the bed. Her mother, coming to visit her, wrote to Parthe: 'She would have made a beautiful sketch, lying there reclining upon pillows in a blue drifting gown, her hair so picturesquely arranged, her expression most trusting, hardly harmonizing with the trenchant things she some-times says, her sweet little hands lying there ready for action.' And action they got. Annotating, tabulating, scribbling, correcting drafts – they were idle only when she slept.

Throughout 1860 Herbert's health continued to deteriorate and before the year's end he knew that he was suffering from an incurable kidney disease. On 5 December 1860 he broke the news to Florence in Hamp-stead – 'not low, but awe-struck'. If he gave up all public work and retired to his beloved Wilton his life might be prolonged, and he would enjoy some leisure with his family in the time that remained.

Torn between a sense of duty and a great weariness, he consulted Florence. It is needless to say that she was on the side of duty. If, at this critical stage, he abandoned the War Office, she knew that everything they had jointly toiled for would go by the board. (Events were to prove her right.) Nor was she, who well knew that doctors were not infallible, prepared to accept their verdict. 'It is *not true*,' she wrote, 'that you cannot (sometimes) mend a damaged organ, almost always keep it comfortably going for many years, by giving Nature fair play. . . . I don't believe there is anything in your constitution which makes it evident that disease is getting the upper hand. On the contrary.'

Even Florence realized, however, that he must reduce the load and that either the House of Commons or the War Office must go. He was a House of Commons man – he had held his seat for twenty-eight years – and hated the War Office with its endless petty-fogging routine. In June 1861 he told her that the work of reform was beyond him. 'The real truth is that I do not understand it. I have not the bump of system in me. I believe more in good men than in good systems.' On days when he spent the morning on a sofa, 'drinking gulps of brandy till I am fit to crawl down to the Office, I am not very energetic when I get there'. As between the War Office and the House of Commons, he was in no doubt. But he also knew, and Florence rammed it home, which way his duty lay. As Minister of War no one could replace him. A dozen half-finished projects would, if he went, be thankfully killed off and buried by Sir Benjamin Hawes. In a letter to Florence he referred to the death of Cavour which had just occurred – 'What a glorious career! What a work done in one life!' and quoted Cavour's last words: '*La cosa va.*' 'That is the life I should like to have lived. That is the death I should like to die.' The outcome of his talk with Florence in December 1860 was that he accepted a peerage (becoming Lord Herbert of Lea), and so was able to continue as the Minister of War.

Until the very last, Florence refused to accept the fact of Herbert's mortal illness. It was too horrible to contemplate: he *must* live until her work was done. In May 1861 she admitted to Liz that he was weaker and thinner, 'yet I don't think him worse in general health, not materially worse'. And in June, to him, 'I believe you have many years of usefulness before you.' But early in July 1861, Herbert's doctors knew the end was near and ordered him to Spa, in Belgium. She accepted his letter of defeat as final and would never speak of it again. 'Many women will not trouble you by breaking their hearts about the organization of an office – that's one comfort. . . . *Hawes has won.*' She offered him no word of comfort. 'A Sidney Herbert beaten by a Ben Hawes is a greater humilia-tion than the disaster of Scutari,' she told him. 'No man in my day has thrown away so noble a game with all the winning cards in his hands.'

He bore no grudge; he had never borne grudges. On 9 July 1861, he called at the Burlington, whither Florence had returned, for a brief goodbye. Four days later he, his wife and a friend, Count Strelecki, reached Spa whither his favourite horse, Andover, had preceded him. He managed to ride every morning until the day before his last at Spa. On the 16th he sent his formal resignation to Palmerston and wrote also to Florence. It was a very business-like letter about a military hospital at Woolwich, and about his successor Sir George Lewis, who would be 'a fish out of water among Armstrong guns and General Officers' but was 'a gentleman, an honest man'. The letter concluded: 'I wish I had any confidence that you are as much better as I am.'

Wilton House, the home of
Sidney Herbert.
RIGHT The south and east
fronts.
BELOW The Double Cube
room.

On 25 July the little party left Spa for Wilton. Even at this eleventh hour, pausing for a night in Brussels, he discussed military hygiene 'eagerly, and at great length' with King Leopold's physician, who left him exclaiming '*Impossible de croire qu'il est si gravement malade!* [Impossible to believe that he is so seriously ill!].' Two days after reaching Wilton, on 2 August 1861, he died peacefully. He was fifty-one. Among his last articulate words, Liz reported, were: 'Poor Florence! Poor Florence! Our joint work unfinished.' And 'I have tried to do my best.'

Poor Florence indeed. She was prostrated and for a month seriously ill. Why had God not 'set aside a few trifling physical laws to save him?' He had been her instrument: 'I cannot do anything without him,' she had written and said over and over again. Now, the instrument broken, he became her 'dear master'. 'Now he takes my life with him,' she wrote to her father. 'My work, the object of my life, the means to it, all in one, depart.' To Harriet Martineau she admitted a hitherto alien prick of remorse for her treatment of Herbert: 'I, too, was hard on him.' 'And his angelic temper with me, at the same time that he felt what I said was true, I shall never forget.'

It was a strange relationship, that between Florence Nightingale, Sidney Herbert and his wife. Day after day, year after year, Herbert and Florence conferred together, dined together, corresponded, on closer terms than many married couples. Both were attractive to the opposite sex. Yet there seems to have been between them never a spark of overt physical attraction, and certainly not the least breath of scandal. Their relationship was wholly intellectual – as she said later, 'exactly like two men'. Even stranger was Liz's attitude. Despite her husband's continual closeting with Florence, despite all the demands Florence made upon him and despite, above all, the way she drove him when he was a sick man, never the least trace of jealousy or resentment clouded their mutual affection. 'A thousand thanks for all you have said and done,' she wrote when Florence persuaded Herbert not to leave the War Office. 'God bless you for all your love and sympathy.' Lytton Strachey wrote that Florence killed Sidney Herbert. This is an exaggeration such as Florence herself might have indulged in; he was killed by a kidney disease. But she may have shortened his life; certainly she kept him from the peace and quiet he could have enjoyed at the end. But: '*la cosa va.*' With that, they both agreed.

Herbert died with his work little more than begun. Most of what he had planned was halted at his death or reversed. Yet even in the short time allowed him, there had been achievements. Some of the worst of the barracks had been condemned, others had been reconditioned, gas laid on instead of 'farthing dips', kitchen ovens provided (thanks also to Soyer), a training-school for cooks established and a start made with providing reading and recreation rooms. During his three years' term of office, the mortality rate in the home army was actually halved. Above all he, as Florence's instrument, had made the public conscious that the health of its army was a matter for public concern: that lives had been thrown away in peacetime which could, and should, have been saved; and between them they had shown how this could be done. Though the armour of official obstruction had been only dented, public apathy was never quite the same again.

The Nightingale
Nurses

THE NIGHTINGALE NURSES

$\mathcal{S}$IDNEY HERBERT'S DEATH was like the loss of a husband, and Florence reacted as a widow by shutting herself away in her rooms and refusing to see most of her friends. People wrote her 'harassing letters', among them Gladstone, who asked for a short account of Herbert's work. He enclosed a sketch by Liz which so irritated Florence – 'there was not one word of truth in it from beginning to end!!!' – that she fell in with Gladstone's wishes and, in a few days, wrote an account of what Herbert had done, and failed to do, for the army. This she had privately printed and circulated. The following year, 1862, it was enlarged and read before the London meeting of the Congrès de Bien-faisance, and published as *Army Sanitary Administration and its Reform under the late Lord Herbert.*

The memoir written, Florence left the Burlington for ever and retreated to her rooms in Hampstead. She kept her address secret and appointed her uncle Sam as her channel of communication with the outside world. For some years this amiable man, who held the office of Examiner of Private Bills, had acted as business manager and to some extent as secretary to his niece. She was lucky to have a tactful and experienced mouthpiece to relay in milder terms such instructions as: 'Please choke off this woman and tell her that I shall *never* be well enough to see her, either here or *hereafter*'; and 'don't let this unbusiness-like woman write any more of these unbusiness-like letters!' On the other hand she was touched by an offer from an upholsterer to make her a couch as 'some

PREVIOUS PAGES The forecourt of St Thomas' Hospital as it was in 1845: drawing by W. Kearney. The original hospital had been founded in medieval times.

slight token of the esteem she is held in by the working-classes for her kindness to our soldiers, many of whom are related to my workmen who would gladly work on her behalf without pay'. Tracts poured in upon her – she detested tracts – with begging letters, poems, cures, inventions (a patent bed-quilt was one) and so many offers of marriage that 'I could have had as many husbands as Mohamet's mother. Alas! it is I who am the grey donkey.' Though gushing, foolish and importunate letter-writers irritated her, she often sent them money, and sometimes Sam Smith added a few pounds of his own.

While Uncle Sam remained a faithful henchman, Aunt Mai defected; and Florence did not forgive her for twenty years. The Smiths' children insisted on their mother's return to a home she had perforce neglected since Scutari days. In her place came Hilary Bonham Carter, but for less than a year. This time Florence herself realized that she was standing in the way of her cousin's artistic development. As a concession she allowed Hilary to make a model of her head and shoulders, one of the few like-nesses she ever sanctioned. In March 1861 Florence told her: 'It would not be right for me any more to absorb your life in letter-writing and housekeeping', and the break was made.

Florence's energies were so stupendous, and her interests so wide, that to chronicle them all in order is impossible. The death of Sidney Herbert provides a convenient point from which to look back. All the time that she was grappling with the reform of the army, she was also pursuing a number of other projects each of which would have fully stretched the capacities of any ordinary hard-working individual.

Hospitals, for a start. Military and civil hospitals did not inhabit different worlds; all were built to a broadly similar design and here, Florence soon decided, lay the root of the trouble. The design was wrong, therefore the nursing was inefficient, therefore the patients suffered and, much too often, died. The hospitals' worst fault lay in lack of ventilation and drainage. In the foul air of damp, unventilated wards, infection spread with deadly speed and virulence. Before bacteria and viruses were discovered, Florence had learned from practical experience to define the conditions which encouraged them to multiply.

Florence had told the Royal Sanitary Commission that she had visited not only all the major hospitals in London, Edinburgh and Dublin, but all those in Paris and Berlin, 'and many others in Germany, at Lyons, Rome, Alexandria, Constantinople, Brussels'. It was in Paris that she learned of the new 'pavilion' design. Its essence was to construct a big hospital in separate units, each unit more or less complete in itself as to kitchens, laundries, ablutions and so on, and each well ventilated, light and airy. By thus avoiding 'the agglomeration of a large number of sick under the same roof', the spread of infection was minimized. Florence became a champion of the 'pavilion' design, and the nub of her objection to the Netley military hospital was its outmoded dependence on corridors.

In October 1858 she expounded her ideas in two papers read to the Social Science Congress at Liverpool. Early in 1859 these were expanded and published in book form as *Notes on Hospitals*. They attracted widespread attention. As usual, no detail was too small for her notice; she championed iron bedsteads (not wood), hair mattresses (not flock), glass or earthenware cups (not tin). To collect the data she had written in her own hand to builders, ironmongers and architects literally in hundreds; one section was headed 'A treatise on sinks'.

The book (108 pages) ran into three editions and established its author as an international authority. Plans for new hospitals were submitted to her by many British cities and boroughs, by the Government of India and by the Queen of Holland. The architect Butterfield was one of her disciples; he built a new infirmary at Winchester on lines she had laid down. The King of Portugal asked her advice about a new hospital in Lisbon. During 1859 and 1860, when her campaign for army reform was at its most exacting, she went to a great deal of trouble to revise the plans. Unfortunately the King had omitted to tell her that it was to be a children's hospital. King Pedro V merely observed that her designs would 'only give the children more room and more air'. Florence was much too meticulous to let this pass, and amended the plans.

In 1859 the South-Eastern Railway sought powers to buy part of the land then occupied by St Thomas' Hospital. The Governors had to decide between selling all the land and rebuilding *de novo* on a new and better site, or selling off what the railway wanted and partially rebuilding on the existing site. The Resident Medical Officer, a Mr Whitfield,

St Thomas' Hospital in 1853: the front quadrangle, with the statue of Edward VI.

sought Florence's advice. She came down in favour of rebuilding on a new site; but some of the Governors thought it would be wrong to move the hospital away from the district it had served for centuries.

Florence was not to be put off with a proposition resting on an assumption. She proceeded to test the assumption statistically. She tabulated and analysed the hospital's records as to where its patients had come from, and showed the assumption to be wrong; a majority lived outside the neighbourhood. Then she drew up tables setting out the extra time and risk involved in taking patients to a more distant hospital, against their chances of recovery in a better building on a healthier site. All this she put into a document which she sent to the Prince Consort, one of the Governors. This carried the day; the whole site was sold to the railway company at the end of 1860 and in due course a new hospital, built on the pavilion plan and completed in 1871, arose on the site in Lambeth where it stands to this day.

Florence had come increasingly to regard statistics not only as the foundation of sanitary reform, but as the source of a keen aesthetic pleasure. What she really liked, she wrote, was to bite on a hard fact. Her interest has been traced back to the work of a Belgian astronomer and statistician, Adolphe Quetelet, who worked out rules for the flowering of plants; the first flowers of the common lilac, he calculated, would appear when the sum of the squares of the mean daily temperatures reckoned from the last frost equalled 4264° C. More weightily, he published in 1835 *Essai de Physique Sociale*, the first work to demonstrate how statistical methods could be applied to social dynamics. This became Florence's bible, and statistics 'the most important science in the whole world'. At Scutari she had found that lack of proper statistics had made it impossible to know exactly how many men had died, let alone from what causes; things were not much better at home. Each hospital had its own system of classifying diseases, so that to arrive at a general picture of the nation's health was impossible. This she set herself to remedy: helped by Dr William Farr, she drew up 'model forms', with a uniform system of classifying diseases, which she had printed, and Dr Farr got them discussed at an International Statistical Congress held in 1860.

As part of her campaign she invited selected foreign delegates to this Congress to a series of breakfasts at the Burlington. Hilary Bonham Carter presided, and she herself received selected guests afterwards in her room upstairs. Even these breakfasts did not escape her extraordinary eye for detail. From her couch came notes to Hilary instructing her to 'take care the cream for breakfast is not turned', and to 'put back Dr X's big book where he can see it drinking his tea'. The 'model forms' duly went to hospitals all over the country and even to Paris, by way of M Mohl. Some adopted them, and used them for several years, but this was one of her reforms that fizzled out, perhaps partly because the medical knowledge on which classification of diseases must be based was too rudimentary for accurate returns.

Sir Edward Cook has suggested that the three people who did most in Britain in the nineteenth century towards alleviating human suffering were Simpson, who introduced chloroform; Lister, who discovered antisepsis; and Florence Nightingale, the founder of modern nursing. We have seen how lowly nurses were regarded at the time of the Crimean War, and how drunken, promiscuous, ignorant and slatternly most of them were. Combined with the horrible state of the hospitals, the ignorance of doctors and the lack of antiseptics, it is indeed a miracle that anyone emerged alive at all. Florence set herself to remedy all this, if not quite singlehanded, always in the van, always the instigator.

LEFT Sir Joseph Lister as President of the Royal Society, in 1897, from a painting by S. Begg. Through his influence in the 1860s and 1870s, the use of antiseptics during surgery was adopted and eventually established.

BELOW Lister's 'Donkey Engine', designed to produce a carbolic spray when the handle was pumped up and down. From Rickman Godlee's biography of Lord Lister, published in 1917.

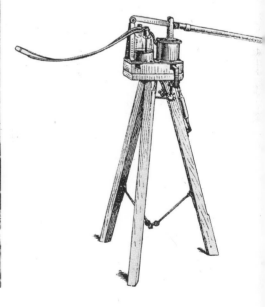

From the construction of hospitals, she turned to the creation of a nursing service of a kind never known in the world before. She had an instrument ready to her hand: the Nightingale Fund, raised in 1855 as a tribute to her own services. This stood at £45,000 and the decision had been taken to spend it on a training-school for female nurses.

When she became involved in the affairs of St Thomas' Hospital, she wrote to Herbert, then president of the Nightingale Fund, suggesting in May 1859 that 'the Matron of that Hospital is the only one of *any existing* Hospital I would recommend to form a "school of instruction" for Nurses. It is not the *best conceivable* way of beginning. But it seems to me to be the *best possible*. It will be beginning in a very humble way.'

The Matron, Mrs Wardroper, was a remarkable woman who had not taken up nursing until widowed, with two children, at the age of forty-two. She had received no training, entered the wards with all their roughness – she was by birth a gentlewoman – and by sheer force of character and competence rose to become Matron in 1853. Florence found that she had raised the standard of nursing at St Thomas' to a level well above that of any other London hospital. She was 'straight-forward, true, upright. She was decided,' Florence wrote, 'free from artificiality and self-interest; her whole heart and mind, her whole life and strength were in the work she had undertaken. She never went a-pleasuring, seldom into society. Yet she was one of the wittiest people one could hear on a summer's day.' Moreover, Mrs Wardroper was willing to take charge of the training experiment, which she warned Florence would provoke from the doctors, for the most part doughty opponents of change, some 'rather harsh criticism'.

At the end of 1859 Florence brought out a short book (seventy-five pages), *Notes on Nursing: What it is, and what it is not*. This proved to be by far her most popular book, as well as the most human, simple and direct, shot through with shafts of her astringent humour based on first-hand-experience, and full of telling asides. Two things she stressed above all others: hygiene, defined as ample fresh air, cleanliness, pure water, proper drainage and plenty of light; and constant consideration for the patient's feelings, in times of sickness so much more sensitive, easily upset and more deserving of sympathy than in times of health.

In this emphasis on the psychological aspects of sickness, she was once again in advance of her time. The least thing, she wrote, can depress, even alarm, a patient: the nurse's cumbrous dress – 'a nurse who rustles is the horror of a patient, though perhaps he does not know why'; sudden jarring sounds – 'unnecessary noise is the most cruel absence of care which can be inflicted'; for example, to 'go on dusting or fidgeting about a sick room all the while the patient is eating, or trying to eat'; even spilling milk or tea into a saucer; 'you have no idea what difference this minute want of care on your part makes to his comfort and even to his willingness for food.' Little things, equally, could aid his recovery; being able to see out of a window; keeping small pets such as a caged bird; a visit from a baby or small child (Florence had been entranced by a visit from her cousin Clough's baby); a piece of good news – 'for instance, of a love and courtship, while in progress to a good ending'. But at all costs, she counselled under the chapter heading 'Chattering Hopes', do not attempt to bolster up the patient by a bright and breezy manner. 'I really believe there is scarcely a greater worry which invalids have to endure than the incurable hopes of their friends.' No one should 'make light of their [the patients'] danger and exaggerate their probabili-ties of recovery'; such 'commonplaces' uttered endlessly by well-meaning persons 'recall the slimy trail left by the snail on the sunny garden-wall loaded with fruit'.

Personal experiences informed every page. 'I shall never forget the rapture of fever patients over a bunch of bright-coloured flowers. I remember in my own case a nosegay of wild flowers being sent me, and from that moment recovery became more rapid.' How little, she wrote, did healthy people who could walk about, take exercise, eat with others, know how much confinement to a sick-room intensified a patient's worries; 'how the very walls of their sick-rooms seem hung with their cares, how the ghosts of their troubles haunt their beds. . . . Remember, he is face to face with his enemy all the time, internally wrestling with him, having long imaginary conversations with him. You are thinking of something else.' Almost every page carries down-to-earth practical hints: 'Never allow a patient to be waked, intentionally, is a *sine qua non* of all good nursing.' 'Never speak to an invalid from behind, nor from

NOTES ON NURSING:

WHAT IT IS, AND WHAT IT IS NOT.

BY

FLORENCE NIGHTINGALE.

LONDON:
HARRISON, 59, PALL MALL,
BOOKSELLER TO THE QUEEN.

The title page of Florence's *Notes on Nursing*, first published in 1859.

the door.' Beef tea and jellies have little nourishment in them; 'the furred tongue almost always likes what is sharp and pungent'; always warm a patient's night-dress before putting it on after his bath; bed-pans *must* be emptied regularly and properly rinsed. 'One word about pillows': do not pile them 'one a-top the other like a wall of bricks', the shoulders should be allowed to fall back and support the head without throwing it forward. 'The suffering of dying patients is immensely increased by neglect of these points.'

No one who reads the little book can doubt that Florence was a compassionate and unselfish nurse. Now and then the tart, critical and above all logical woman breaks through: 'No *man*, not even a doctor, ever gives any other definition of what a nurse should be than this – "devoted and obedient". This definition would do just as well for a porter. It might even do for a horse. It would not do for a policeman.' She herself wrote that the best definition of a nurse 'was to be found, as always, in Shakespeare':

> So kind, so duteous, diligent,
> So tender over his occasions, true,
> So feat, so nurse-like.
> *(Cymbeline)*

And finally, on a still controversial topic:

I would earnestly ask my sisters to keep clear of both the jargons now current everywhere, of the jargon, namely, about the 'rights of women', which urges women to do all that men do, merely because men do it, and without regard to whether this *is* the best thing women can do; and the jargon which urges women to do nothing that men do, merely because they are women, and should be 'recalled to a sense of their duty as women' . . . and 'these are things women should not do', which is all assertion and nothing more. Surely woman should bring the best she has, *whatever* that is, to the work of God's world, without attending to either of these cries.

In other words, no Women's Lib, but no Woman's Place is the Home either: let us forget about sex when it comes to the use of human talent and let every he or she contribute what is in them to achieve. Surely, in 1860, so forward-looking an attitude that it has yet to become general in 1975. She ended her book: 'Oh, let us leave these jargons, and go your way straight to God's work, in simplicity and singleness of heart.'

Notes on Nursing was an immediate success. From the Queen downwards, it was praised by all. Though published at five shillings, a high price in those days, it quickly sold fifteen thousand copies and went into several cheap editions, was translated into foreign languages and printed in America.

Its publication was followed by the opening of the Nightingale Training School for Nurses at St Thomas' Hospital on 24 June 1860. It started with fifteen probationers, chosen with great care and by no means easily found. One floor of a new wing was set aside for them; each probationer had a room to herself and the use of communal sitting-rooms; their Supervisor had her apartment on the same floor, and their board, uniform and laundry were provided for them, plus £10 a year pocket-money and a bonus of £5 or £3, according to proficiency, on qualifying at the end of the year. They wore a simple and, in its day, becoming brown uniform with white caps and aprons.

All this was new, indeed revolutionary. So was the other main principle of the School, that the students should receive the best technical training available, both from Sisters in the wards and from surgeons and physicians. Three senior members of the medical staff agreed to give lectures, and for the first time probationers were instructed in the scientific basis of their work. At the end of their course, their names were to be placed on a Register of Certified Nurses – the seed of the future roll of State Registered Nurses.

There was, of course, medical opposition. St Thomas' had its own Dr Hall in the person of Mr J. F. South, the senior surgeon and twice President of the Royal College of Surgeons. He did not think there was room for much improvement in existing methods, and in any case nurses were 'in much the same position as housemaids, and require little teaching beyond that of poultice-making'. In a pamphlet written to deride proposals for reform, Mr South let out of his black bag a distinctly spiteful pussy. 'That this proposed hospital training scheme has not met with the approbation or support of the medical profession is beyond doubt. The very small number whose names appear in the enormous list of subscribers to the Nightingale Fund cannot have passed unnoticed.

Only three physicians and one surgeon from one London hospital and one physician from a second are found among the supporters.' Fortunately she had powerful allies, including Mr Whitfield, the royal physician Sir James Clark and Sir James Paget, senior surgeon at St Bartholomew's.

The first fifteen 'Nightingale nurses' began their training in a missionary atmosphere. Few students can have been more closely shepherded. Florence drew up a 'Monthly Sheet of Personal Character and Acquirements' in two parts. One, the Moral Record, had subheads to assess the probationers' score for punctuality, quietness, trustworthiness, personal neatness and cleanliness, and ward management. The Technical Record had no less than fourteen heads, some of them sub-divided, and there were five grades in marking: Excellent, Good, Moderate, Imperfect and Nil. Mrs Wardroper added her personal comments. No minor failing – nor, one must hope, success – escaped notice. One of the girls 'uses her eyes unpleasantly'; with age, Mrs Wardroper hoped, 'this failing – an unfortunate one – may possibly decrease'. A girl caught out in a flirtation with a medical student was sacked. Probationers were required to go out in pairs, never singly, but the old Eve crept in; 'of course we parted when we got to the corner,' one of them later confessed.

The School was an immediate success. Thirteen out of the fifteen probationers qualified and were employed by hospitals and infirmaries – private nursing was discouraged. Soon demand greatly exceeded supply. Part of the Fund was then used to start the training of midwives. 'In nearly every country but our own there is a Government School for Midwives,' Florence wrote. 'I trust that our School may lead the way towards supplying a want long felt in England.' At first it did; but after six successful years there was an outbreak of puerperal fever and it had to be closed. Nevertheless, schools both for nurses and for midwives caught on, and from that small acorn grew the present oak of training for the nursing profession all over the world.

As if all this were not enough to keep Florence occupied – her life was still believed to be hanging by a thread – it was at this time, in 1860, that she circulated to a number of friends the lengthy draft of a work of dense theological and philosophical argument. Its origins went back to

Mrs Wardroper, Matron of St Thomas', and superintendent of the Nightingale Training School for Nurses. Florence considered her to be the only woman to take charge of this crucial experiment designed to create a new kind of nursing service.

1851 when she had reached a nadir of frustration, unhappiness and doubt, and her distraught mind, sick for certainty, was receiving a dusty answer from the dogmas of religion. She had struggled to re-think the precepts hitherto accepted about God – there was no question of her abandoning the concept altogether – and to arrive at 'a new religion', or at any rate a form of religion in which she could fully believe.

Her principal mentors were Edgar Quinet, author of *Histoire de mes Idées*, and J. S. Mill. On her thirty-second birthday, on 12 May 1852, she had written to her father of the 'beautiful arrangement of Infinite Wisdom, which cannot create us gods, but which will not create us animals, and therefore wills mankind to create mankind by their own experience'. She added that she would be very glad to read to him, at breakfast, 'any of my "Works", if you have any desire to hear them'. These 'Works', subsequently called by her 'the Stuff', were dedicated to 'the Artizans of England'.

In 1851, a year after the publication of Charles Kingsley's *Alton Locke, Tailor and Poet*, she had jotted down a resolution to devote part of her life to devising a 'new religion for the tailors'. This, in effect, was it, although to have received the message they would have needed to be very studious tailors indeed.

The *opus*, expanded, revised and titled *Suggestions for Thought*, was sent to two men whom she greatly revered but had never met: J. S. Mill and the future Master of Balliol, Benjamin Jowett. She asked for their frank opinions and received conflicting replies. J. S. Mill wrote that he had 'seldom felt less inclined to criticize than in reading this book', and strongly advised her to publish it. But Jowett, though in some ways scarcely less enthusiastic – 'it seemed to me as if I had received the impress of a new mind' – advised against publication in its existing form; he thought it too disorganized and diffuse.

It was strange that Florence, as a rule so orderly, logical and intolerant of sloppiness, should in her own most personal work have been faulted on these grounds. She had never been able to give it proper attention. A new theological and philosophical system of thought cannot be constructed in odd moments spared from a full life of action. Most of her advisers counselled against publication in its existing form and wanted her to shorten, recast and revise it. She compromised by having it privately printed as it stood, in three large volumes and 829 pages. The artisans therefore remained uninstructed, but it brought its author a new and rewarding relationship. Until Jowett's death in 1893 they remained close friends, indeed it was said that he wanted to marry her.

'This book is written by an infidel who has been a Papist,' was one of his comments. She had never been either, keeping to her resolve not to 'be smothered in the dust raised by these religious hoofs'. Orthodox religions seemed to her inseparable from cant, and it was cant that she despised above all. 'Is there anything higher in thinking of one's own salvation than in thinking of one's own dinner?' She was no Evangelical. The soldier who gave his life for 'something other than his own shilling' was higher in the scale than those who saw their own salvation as the end of their religion. She herself reached out, albeit wordily, towards a kind of mysticism based on the ancient truth that God is love. 'It is not the material presence only that we love in our fellow creatures. It is the spirit, which bespeaks the material presence, that we love. Shall we not then love the spirit of all that is lovable . . .?' Hers was a passionate nature with a great store of love, her life a search for objects – family, friends, heroes, disciples, categories of people – on whom to bestow it.

Towards the end of 1861 she accepted an offer by her brother-in-law Sir Harry Verney of the use of his house in South Street, and moved there with her retinue of cats – a move from one sofa to another. She was still in mourning for her 'dear Master'. 'It is as if the earth had opened up and swallowed up even the Name which filled my whole life these five years.' Soon after her move came another blow, almost as shattering as 'the Master's' demise, the death of Arthur Clough. She fell into a state of utter despondency. The delivery of all newspapers stopped, lest she should read in them of the death of yet another friend. To Mary Mohl she wrote: 'I do believe that I am "like a man" as Parthe says. But how? *In having sympathy*. I am sure I have nothing else. I am sure that my contemporaries, Parthe, Hilary, Marianne, Lady Dunsany, were all cleverer than I was, and several of them more unselfish. But not one had a bit of sympathy. . . .' In her illness and isolation she was engulfed in waves of self-pity:

People often say to me, You don't know what a wife and mother feels. No, I say, I don't and I am very glad I don't. And *they* don't know what *I feel*. . . . Ezekiel went running about naked, 'for a sign'. I can't run about naked because it is not the custom of the country. But I would mount three widows' caps on my head, 'for a sign'. And I would cry, This is for Sidney Herbert, this is for Arthur Clough, and This, the biggest widow's cap of all, is for the loss of all sympathy on the part of my nearest and dearest. . . . [She was referring to her aunt Mai.]

Once again she thought she was dying, and two doctors were in attendance. 'I am glad to end a day which can never come back', she wrote to her mother, 'gladder to end a night, gladdest to end a month.' She had thought Liz Herbert childish when she said that she had found her greatest comfort 'in a little Chinese dog of his, which he was not very fond of either', and which had licked the tears from her cheek, 'but now I don't. My cat does just the same to me. Dumb beasts observe you so much more than talking beings. . . .' Even if she lived, she believed that her usefulness was over. 'She thinks she may withdraw her hand from Government matters entirely,' Hilary Bonham Carter wrote.

Before the year was out, her hand was back once more in its accustomed position at the remote controls. The American Civil War had started and British troops were to be sent to Canada in case Britain became involved. Herbert had been succeeded by Sir George Lewis, with whom Florence felt little sympathy as she used the term, in the sense of being *simpatico*; but with the Under-Secretary, Lord de Grey, she was much more *en rapport*. He wrote for her advice 'as to sanitary arrangements generally' for the expeditionary force.

This scent of battle could not be resisted by the seasoned war-horse. Without a moment's delay, she summoned Dr Sutherland and between them they revised the draft instructions to the officers in charge which de Grey had sent her. Methods of distributing the meat and clothing had not been properly defined; without precision, 'you will have men, as you had in the Crimea, shirking the responsibility.' What distances could sledges average in a day? What were the relative weights and warmth of blankets and buffalo robes? Florence worked out these and innumerable other details. 'We are shipping off the Expedition to

Clara Barton, founder of the American Red Cross. Improvements in medicine were spreading throughout the Continent and North America, and each nation had its heroines among the newly developing nursing profession, often to be found on the world's battlefields.

Canada as fast as we can,' she wrote exultantly to Mary Mohl from South Street on 13 December 1861. 'I have been working just as I did in the times of Sidney Herbert. Alas! he left no organization, my dear master!'

Once back on the battle-field, the war-horse gradually recovered strength; if only to the point where death receded; for the rest of her life, which still had nearly fifty years to run, she remained an invalid, and for the next six years had to be carried from room to room and never went out of doors. 'I never see the spring without thinking of my Clough. He used to tell me how the leaves were coming out – always remembering that, without his eyes, I should never see the spring again.' Insofar as this was possible, the seasons came to her, and her rooms were always filled with flowers. But blue books, reports from the Registrar-General, abstracts, columns of statistics, more and more filled her life. 'A great Commander was lost to her country when Florence Nightingale was born a woman,' wrote Sir Edward Cook. Instead, Commanders came to her, sat at her feet and took their instructions.

After Canada recalled her to duty, India occupied her attention. In 1858 she wrote on the fly-leaf of her *Notes on the Army*: 'The British race has carried with it into those regions of the sun [India] its habits, its customs and its vices, without considering that under a low temperature man may do with impunity what under a higher one is death.' She had put her finger on the root cause of appallingly high mortality from sickness, even higher than at home, among British troops in India. Men were expected to drill for hours on shadeless barrack squares in the hottest weather, and to dwell in sweltering and stinking cantonments, in the same uniform, on the same diet and in the same sardine-packed conditions as those which they endured in British winters. In 1859 it was revealed that the average death-rate among British soldiers serving in India during the past forty years had been sixty-nine per thousand, compared with 17·5 per thousand in the Knightsbridge barracks.

Among Florence's influential friends was Lord Stanley, later fifteenth Earl of Derby, the Prime Minister's son. He sent her Government papers, solicited her advice and sometimes asked questions that she wanted asked in the House of Commons. In 1858 he became Secretary of State for India. For some little time a new project had been forming in Florence's mind: the appointment of a Royal Commission to do for the troops in India what the Royal Sanitary Commission had just done for the troops in Britain. This seemed the moment to press it on Lord Derby. She spent eight months, she wrote to Harriet Martineau, 'importunate-widowing' him, and in May 1859 announced triumphantly 'We have just won it. The Queen has signed the Warrant. So it is safe.' Among the members were her four faithful doctors: Sutherland, Farr, Martin and Alexander. After a change of Government, the Chair was taken by Lord Stanley himself. The name of the Commission's most active,

Harriet Martineau in 1849: a portrait in chalk by George Richmond. Lacking in personal charm – Charlotte Brontë found her rigid daily routine formidable – Harriet Martineau was nevertheless a woman of great influence, and one of the nineteenth century's outstanding feminists. As leader-writer of the *Daily News*, she was well placed to rally support for Florence's various causes, and numbered among her friends Gladstone, Carlyle, Bulwer Lytton and Lord Brougham.

influential and indefatigable participant did not appear among the list of members. This, of course, was that of Miss Nightingale.

Even before the Warrant was signed, she had started the enormous task of assembling the needed data. With Sutherland and Farr, she set about statistic-gathering from every Indian station and cantonment where British troops were to be found. The task was particularly complicated because India still had two British armies, that of the Queen and that of the East India Company. The latter was in the process of being absorbed into the former, but such statistics as there were had formerly been separately collected, and the Company's affairs were in some confusion. There was only one way to tackle the matter and that was to send directly to every military station – about two hundred – in India a 'circular of enquiry', and to write individually to all senior medical and army authorities. This Florence proceeded to do. The Commission never visited India. It stayed at home digesting figures like a mighty boa-constrictor, with Florence, Sutherland and Farr performing the function, one might say, of its insatiable stomach.

The outcome was a truly formidable document: two volumes of small print totalling 2,028 pages, published in 1863. 'The greater part', wrote Sir Edward Cook, 'bears in one way or another the impress of Miss Nightingale.' The whole of the second volume (959 pages) consisted of replies to her enquiries from India, all of which had gone direct to her to be analysed. Her annual hegira from Mayfair to Hampstead and back again was accompanied by van-loads of documents. No comparable study of Indian conditions had ever before been attempted, and it was ten years before an official survey was made.

In October 1861 the Commission had invited Florence to submit her observations on the Station reports. She did so in twenty-three pages. She knew perfectly well that no one was going to read two thousand pages of small type. But they would read twenty-three brisk pages by Miss Nightingale, especially as she baited the trap with a series of woodcuts done by Hilary Bonham Carter. This was something altogether new in blue books; the Treasury naturally demurred, but Florence undertook to pay the extra cost herself. She had her *Observations* privately printed and sent to everyone of influence she knew, including the Queen, remarking that 'she may look at it because it has pictures.'

A great many people looked at it, not only for the pictures but because it revealed a shocking state of affairs. No one had previously bothered to find out the dreadful conditions under which the British troops in India lived. The higher death and sickness rate was generally put down to tropical diseases, but Florence showed that the main causes were the same as in the Crimea: badly selected camp sites, bad drainage, contaminated water, overcrowding, unsanitary buildings, poor ventilation and hopelessly unsuitable diets – the whole devil's brew of avoidable sickness and death concocted by the hags of ignorance, indifference and incompetence. The proximity of crowded Indian towns where disease was rife and sewerage unknown exacerbated matters. Refuse flung into the streets was never cleared, corpses were buried within the precincts of houses, animals rotted where they died, scavenging was left to crows and pi-dogs. Native towns had been allowed to grow up in the cantonments: at Bangalore a hundred thousand Indians lived within the army precincts. In some Stations three hundred soldiers slept in one room. Drinking water 'visibly swarmed with animal life'. Sometimes there was nothing for the men to wash in or, if there was, the allowance of one basin to a hundred men. There were no recreation rooms, no libraries, no sports grounds. Troops were often confined to barracks in the stifling heat between 8 a.m. and 5 p.m.

A female sweeper: one of the woodcuts made by Hilary Bonham Carter for Florence's *Observations on the Sanitary State of the Army in India.*

Married quarters were even worse. In one province, one soldier's child in five survived into its sixth year. The only thing they seemed to have enough of was gut-rotting liquor. 'If facilities for washing were as great as those for drink,' Florence commented, 'our Indian army would be the cleanest body of men in the world.' She added: 'The men are killed by liver disease on canteen spirits to save them from being killed by liver disease on bazaar spirits. May there not be some middle course whereby the men may be killed by neither?'

The conclusion she drew from these discoveries was that one could not improve the health of British troops in India without introducing at least some rudimentary improvements in the general health, housing and cleanliness of the Indian population. It was all of one piece. 'The salvation of the Indian army must be brought about by sanitary measures everywhere,' she wrote; a frightening conclusion, but it had to be faced.

On 19 May 1863, just four years after the Commission's appointment, she wrote to Harriet Martineau: 'I cannot help telling you in the joy of my heart that the final meeting of the Indian Sanitary Commission was held today – that the Report was signed and that, after a very tough fight, lasting over three days to convince these people that a report was not self-executive, our working commission was carried.' The working commission was to see that the report would not be still-born.

At no time in her life did Florence work harder than during those four years. It was sheer grinding, detailed paper-work lacking the drama and humanity that had sustained her at Scutari. The nurse had turned

'The Indian drainage system', another of Hilary Bonham Carter's woodcuts for the *Observations*.

INDIAN DRAINAGE SYSTEM.

'Daily means of occupation and amusement': this woodcut by Hilary Bonham Carter (from *Observations*) illustrates the lack of leisure-time activities for the ordinary soldier, who led an unhealthy life with very little exercise.

statistician. She enjoyed no relaxations, and had few intimate friends beyond her cats; her family had in her view deserted her; she was weak and subject to frequent headaches and palpitations. Yet she drove herself on and on. Why? For all her volubility on paper, she left no clue beyond a sense of duty that had become inflamed. All around she saw her Master's work undone, at best unfinished. Others had failed him. At least there would be one disciple who would carry to its conclusion the Master's work in such a fashion as to comply with the exacting standards to which his life had been sacrificed.

Even for Florence, there were compensations. Her work brought her new friends who, if they could never replace the old, satisfied her need to love, respect and serve a man as well as a cause. All the men who won her admiration were men of character. The character of Sir John

Lawrence was very different from that of such sensitive and cultured individuals as Herbert and Clough. But all shared, she later wrote, the 'one thing needful' – 'the serving with all their souls and minds and without a thought of self their high idea of right'. They shared also physical good looks: Lawrence was tall, fair-haired, with piercing blue eyes and a craggy handsomeness, tough and incorruptible, resolute and brave, a puritan and intensely religious. One of a family of twelve born to an Ulster Protestant officer, he was brought up in the strictest discipline and austerity – at school he was flogged every day of his life, he said, except one, when he was flogged twice. He was, in some ways, a rough diamond, 'more like a navvy than a gentleman' according to a colleague; 'an old bullock for work' according to himself.

He and Florence had a lot in common: a passion for work, absolute rectitude, religious belief, ruthless efficiency, a thirst for facts and underneath, a genuine sympathy for the native peoples. 'One *lakh* given in the reduction of tax assessments and making people comfortable in their homes is better than three *lakhs* given to Rajas,' was a remark that Florence herself might have made.

Soon after the Commission's report was published, the current Viceroy died suddenly, and Sir John Lawrence was appointed to succeed him. Lord Derby, by now a convinced sanitarian, thought that Lawrence needed further briefing. He wrote to Florence on 1 December 1863, 'Why should he not see you? The plans are in the main yours; no one can explain them better; you have been in frequent correspondence with him. I believe there will now be but little difficulty in India. . . . Let me repeat – you must manage to see Sir John Lawrence.'

She did. Years later she wrote: 'He came like a footman to my door without giving his name. . . . The interview was one never to be forgotten.' It was solely concerned, we need hardly say, with Indian sanitary matters, and before the end Sir John was heart and soul her man. 'So far from considering our Report exaggerated,' she wrote delightedly to Dr Farr, 'he considers it under the mark.' Within a month of his return to India, Sir John had set up Sanitary Committees for Calcutta, Madras and Bombay. He wrote to Florence: 'I hope that you will expedite the transmission to India of the codes and rules and plans which have been

OPPOSITE *Awaiting Admission to the Casualty Ward* by the Pre-Raphaelite artist Luke Fildes. Hospital conditions, though improved, still had a long way to go. This painting is at the Royal Holloway College.

approved of for home and the colonies.' He added: 'Where we differ, it will become our duty to set forth the grounds for so doing, in sending our plans and reports home.' This was a remarkable statement from a blunt and autocratic Viceroy who had served in India for over thirty years, to an invalid spinster with no official position, who had never been to India at all. 'Men used to say,' Sir Bartle Frere subsequently recalled, 'that they always knew when the Viceroy had received a letter from

Sir John Lawrence, the man on whom Florence relied to carry out her reforms in India. Although his achievements fell short of her expectations, under his Viceroyship the judicial system was reformed, forestry departments created and railways extended.

Florence Nightingale: it was like the ringing of a bell to call for sanitary progress.'

'I am doing what I can to put things in order out here,' the Viceroy wrote to her, 'but it is very uphill work.' In her replies Florence grew ecstatic, almost hysterical in her praise.

I always feel that you are the greatest figure in history, and yours the greatest work in history in modern times. . . . We have but one Sir John Lawrence. . . . Health is the product of a civilization, i.e. of real civilization. In Europe we have a kind of civilization to proceed upon. In India your work represents, not only diminished Mortality as with us, but increase of energy, increase of power of the populations. I always feel, as if God had said: mankind is to create mankind. In this sense you are the greatest creator of mankind in modern history. . . . Would there be any impropriety in your Sanitary Com/ missions sending copies of their printed Minutes to the Barrack and Hospital Improvement Commission here?

She went on to advise him how to deal with 'three glaring (tho' lesser) evils in Calcutta' – police hospitals, jails and lunatic asylums, and seamen at the ports. Immured in her room in South Street, India stretched before her mind's eye, a great panorama of villages in need of pure water, drainage and latrines, of teeming populations crying out for decent food, ventilated houses, medical care. 'Oh that I could come out to Calcutta and organize at least the Hospital accommodation for the poor wretches in the streets,' she wrote to Lawrence. Alas, that it was impossible; but at least there was a Lawrence in command 'conquering India anew by civilization, taking possession of the Empire for the first time by knowledge instead of by the sword'. 'I sing for joy every day,' she wrote, 'at Sir John Lawrence's Government.'

The song faded. Under Lawrence's rule little was accomplished in India after all; but when he returned, she wrote that 'all the statesmen in England whether "in" or "out" seem to me like rats or weazels compared to him.' Those in whom she could sense nothing worshipful, she could not love. That was why she did less than justice to Dr Sutherland, so devoted, so indispensable. He gave his whole life to her yet he lacked this spark of moral grandeur and merely irritated her with his fussiness, his unbusiness/like habits, his growing deafness, his unpunctuality. The

OPPOSITE Excavating on the Westminster site designated for the new building of St Thomas' Hospital. A watercolour in the possession of the Greater London Council.

singleness of purpose that she looked for she did not find in him.

Just as a Little War Office had established itself at the Burlington Hotel, so a Little India Office came into being at 32, South Street. The president of the Madras Sanitary Commission made his headquarters there and Florence organized his tours of hospitals and barracks. The Viceroy sent her drafts of proposed legislation for criticism, and she composed and had printed documents such as one entitled: 'Note on the relations which should exist between the powers of raising and spending taxes proposed to be granted to local authorities, and the proper execution of sanitary works and measures in India.' No wonder she complained to Julius Mohl, writing on the first day of 1864, 'I have done nothing else for seven years except write Regulations.' No wonder she had felt 'an awful wreck' for three years. 'I don't think I have much more work in me,' she had written at the end of 1863. But work poured in. She was still struggling to put the Army Medical School on the right lines. 'I wrote *for the tenth time* a statement of eight pages,' she told Sir James Clark.

Once again, no detail was too small: warrants for apothecaries, appointment of staff surgeons for the West Indies, an outbreak of yellow fever in Bermuda, victualling on transports, how an 'iron house' at Aldershot should be used – for a soldiers' recreation room, as the War Office wanted, or for an officers' club as proposed by the Horse Guards. Florence rallied Parliamentary support and the recreation party won; then she framed a set of Regulations for reading-rooms and listed the appropriate furniture and fittings. 'We may not hope to make saints of all,' she wrote of the soldiers, 'but we can make men of them instead of brutes.' She even paid attention to the comfort of their horses. The design of the new loose-boxes for the cavalry found its way to South Street. They ought to have windows, she told her cousin's husband Captain Douglas Galton, now in a senior position at the War Office. 'I do not speak from hearsay but from actual personal acquaintance with horses of an intimate kind.' It was of the utmost importance to their health and spirits to be able to see out. 'I have told Dr Sutherland but he has no feeling.' Dr Sutherland retorted that windows *had* been included in the design and 'every horse can see out if he chooses to stand on his hind legs with his forefeet against the wall.' If her theory was correct, he added, this was the least the horse could do for his own good.

The long-suffering doctor got into serious trouble when, in 1865, there was talk of sending him to report on an outbreak of cholera in the Mediterranean stations. 'For God's sake, if you can,' she appealed to Galton, 'prevent Dr Sutherland going.' Not only did he lack feeling, 'he is so childish that if he heard of this Malta and Gibraltar business he would instantly declare there was nothing to keep him in England.' Owing to his deafness, she had taken to communicating with him mainly in peremptory little notes on scraps of paper. 'Can you answer a plain question?' 'You have forgotten all we talked about.' 'Why did you tell me that tremendous *banger*? Was it to prevent my worrying you?' In the doctor's *ripostes* there was sometimes a flash of rueful humour. He drew a picture of a pump with its handle labelled 'FN'. 'Your pump is dry. India to stand over.' At the end of 1865 he and his wife moved further out of London to Norwood, where he took up gardening. 'He always has some *pond* to dig,' she wrote. 'Confound that Norwood.'

One step Florence could, and did, take to lighten the load was to refuse to see all visitors except a very few close friends and relatives, and those directly engaged on pressing mutual business. A visitor admitted to the house was given a pencil and paper and asked to state his business. The message was taken to the unseen presence upstairs and in due course back came an answer, brief and to the point. That was all. She made no concessions. Regretfully, she refused to see the Queen of Holland: 'She is a Queen of Queens. But it is quite, quite, quite, impossible.' Florence's oldest, closest friend was 'Clarkey' Mohl. They corresponded frequently, at length and in the most affectionate terms. In June 1865 Mary Mohl came to London and Florence refused to see even her. This, too, was 'quite, quite, quite impossible. I am sure no one ever gave up so much to live who longed so much to die as I do and give up daily.' In October she wrote, also to 'Clarkey', 'I am so weak, no one knows how weak I am.' Because she had seen Dr Sutherland for a few minutes, and then had a few more minutes with 'my good Mrs Sutherland', she was 'with a spasm of heart' until the next morning and 'nearly unfit for work all today'.

Number 10 South Street, Park Lane – the house in the centre with the balcony: this was Florence's town house from 1865 until her death. It has since been demolished.

The year 1865 brought another personal blow. Ever since she had sent away her cousin Hilary in the interests of Hilary's career, the two women had seen little of each other; and Hilary, far from being freed to develop her talents, had become virtually a domestic slave – 'devoured by little black relations just like fleas', wrote Mary Mohl. In May 1865, after dreadful suffering, she died of cancer. Florence's bitter grief was mixed with rage against the waste of talent and against the selfishness of Hilary's family. It recalled her own treatment, and the wound broke out afresh. Even her favourite cat, she wrote to Mary Mohl, 'seemed to know something was wrong the day Hilary died and sat with his arms round my neck. Whereas Parthe e.g., never said one word but of hardness to me in all my trial years.' She was being unjust, and Jowett, to whom also she poured out her miseries, gently told her so. They had become constant and affectionate correspondents and he came to South Street on several occasions to administer the Sacrament. He advised her to carry on her work 'not with less energy, but in a calmer spirit'.

At least she now had a house of her own: number 35, later re-numbered number 10, South Street, bought by her father in a somewhat grudging spirit. Flo was an expensive daughter, and he had Lea Hurst and Embley to keep up. He paid £5,000 for the freehold plus £2,000 contributed by Fanny. 'Of course I shall consider the money sunk from the time I produce it,' he wrote grumpily, 'and shall hope *never to hear any more of it.*' In October 1865 she moved in and made her home there for the rest of her life. At the back was the garden of Dorchester House, with its trees and grass and the birds she loved observing. Sometimes half a dozen cats roamed about the house at will, often leaving paw-marks on her papers.

The winter of 1865–6 was a bad one. In addition to her heart condition, she suffered from severe back pains diagnosed as 'rheumatism of the spine'. Massage did no good, but 'a curious little new-fangled operation of putting opium under the skin' brought relief for twenty-four hours at the price of fuddling her brain. She could not sleep and took again to serious reading: Plato in Greek, Mme Roland's *Memoires*, *Atlanta in Calydon*. To make matters worse, Dr Sutherland, as she had feared, escaped to Gibraltar and Malta; and while he was away a crisis blew up. A despatch from Lawrence vital to her plans for Indian reform was mislaid in the India Office for nearly four months. Before her scheme for an Indian public health system, based on this despatch, could be approved, the Whig Government fell. She was too late by twenty-four hours. 'I am furious to that degree . . . that I am fit to blow you all to pieces with an infernal machine,' she wrote to Galton. Such an opportunity never came again.

Governess
of India

CHAPTER EIGHT

GOVERNESS OF INDIA

IN THE SUMMER OF 1866 Florence visited Embley for the first time in ten years. She travelled in an invalid carriage and stayed for three and a half months. Her mother was now seventy-eight and going blind. 'I don't think my dear mother was ever more touching and interesting to me than now she is in her state of dilapidation,' she wrote to Mary Mohl. 'She is much gentler, calmer, more thoughtful.' Relatives who came to Embley found Florence difficult and critical. They dared not 'explain anything to Flo' because her heart 'may *snap* at any extra effort or excitement'. It was perhaps a relief to everyone when Flo returned to South Street in November to gird herself anew for the fray. She did not cease from strife nor go out of her house for thirteen months.

First there was India. Sir John Lawrence was proving a broken reed. The health commissions he had set up in the main provinces had been whittled away. The India Office had a new and unknown chief, Sir Stafford Northcote. 'Our Indian affairs are getting as drunk as they can be,' she wrote to Galton. He advised her to see Sir Bartle Frere, who had just completed his term as Governor of Bombay and become a member of the India Council in London. He came to South Street in June 1867 and they conquered each other. He became one of the most ardent converts to her cause.

As long ago as 1860 she had written to Frere: 'Bombay has a lower death-rate in the last two years than London, the healthiest city in Europe. This is entirely your doing. If we do not take care, Bombay will

PREVIOUS PAGES
Parthenope, Florence and Sir Harry Verney photographed at Claydon in their old age. Despite their life-long rivalry, Florence showed great patience in looking after Parthe, who for the last seven years of her life was crippled with arthritis. 'You contributed more than anyone to what enjoyment of life was hers,' Sir Harry wrote to her.

214

Sir Bartle Frere: another of Florence's dedicated disciples. Like Lawrence, he spent a long career in the service of the Government in India, and as Governor of Bombay won the sympathy of his subjects. He founded a school for the daughters of Indian gentlemen, and Indians as well as Europeans were welcomed at Government House.

outstrip us in the sanitary race. People will be ordered for the benefit of their health to Bombay. . . .' 'I need not tell you how entirely my services are at your disposal,' he wrote to her.

'If only we could get a Public Health Department in the India Office to ourselves with Sir B. Frere at the head of it, our fortunes would be made,' she wrote to Galton in July. She had drawn up a detailed plan for the administration of a public health service throughout India. Her next step towards its adoption must be to talk over Sir Stafford Northcote, the new Secretary of State. The meeting took place on 20 August 1867 and was a great success. 'I don't know that he saw how afraid I was of him,' she told Dr Sutherland. 'For he kept his eyes tight shut all the time. And I kept mine wide open.' She kept her wits alert also, and by the end of an hour's talk, a 'controlling committee' at the India Office with Sir Bartle Frere in charge was settled. 'I wish I could choose the members as I did in Sidney Herbert's time,' she wrote to Galton. She never could forget her Master; on a letter of Sir Bartle Frere's she scribbled, 'I miss him so.' On every anniversary of his death she shut herself away and spent the day in meditation and prayer.

In October 1867 Stafford Northcote called again 'to be coached in the best way to announce the Sanitary Committee to the War Office'. She was back in the saddle again. Back, it might be said, in several saddles. In 1861 William Rathbone, head of a well-known Liverpool family of ship-owners, had conceived the idea of employing nurses to help the sick poor in their own homes. He quickly discovered that trained nurses were not to be found, and wrote to Florence. The only way to get nurses, she replied, was to start a training school in Liverpool on the same lines as the Nightingale School at St Thomas'. This was done, at Rathbone's own expense, the following year.

The lot of the sick poor in their slum homes was bad enough but worse still was the lot of sick paupers in the Workhouse Infirmary. This contained between a thousand and fifteen hundred destitute, homeless creatures of all ages, suffering from almost every ailment under the sun, bundled together into filthy, ill-ventilated wards which had to be patrolled at night by policemen. In the whole Infirmary there was not a single trained nurse. Female paupers were supposed to nurse their fellow-paupers. Most of them were drunken prostitutes. The blankets and such clothing as the paupers had were scarcely ever washed, nor the wards cleaned. Food was purloined, suffering left unrelieved and deathbeds unattended. When parish officials inspected the wards, they wore gloves for protection. It was, said Florence, 'Scutari over again'.

Early in 1864 William Rathbone sent Florence the outline of a plan for introducing a staff of trained nurses headed by a Lady Superintendent, to be paid for by himself. Florence, aided as ever by Dr Sutherland, set to work at once on the practical details. Twelve Nightingale nurses would be sent from St Thomas' and luckily she knew the very person to fill the post of Superintendent, Miss Agnes Jones. Like Florence, she was by birth a gentlewoman, in fact a niece of Sir John Lawrence. She had even, like Florence also, worked at Kaiserswerth before enrolling at St Thomas', where she was said to have been the best pupil Mrs Wardroper ever had. Florence described her to Mary Mohl as 'pretty and young and rich and witty, ideal in her beauty as a Louis XIV shepherdess'. Mrs Wardroper found her trustworthy, methodical, intelligent and an excellent moral influence on others. She was deeply religious. In 1864, at the age of thirty-two, she accepted the post of Superintendent at the Liverpool Infirmary and with a band of twelve nurses started work in May 1865. May was also the month of Florence's birthday, and William Rathbone wrote asking 'to be allowed to constitute myself your gardener to the extent of doing what I have long wished – providing a flower-stand for your room and keeping it supplied with plants'. This he did until his death, in gratitude for having 'guided me to and in this work'.

The wards at the Workhouse Infirmary were likened by Agnes Jones to Dante's Inferno. Even after her experience in London hospitals, 'she did not know,' Florence wrote, 'what sin and wickedness were. Vicious habits, ignorance, idiocy, met her on every side. Drunkenness was universal – thirty-five of the pauper nurses had to be dismissed for drunkenness in the first month.' (They were considered drunk only when unable to stand; lesser degrees did not count.) 'Immorality was universal. Filth was universal; food was at starvation level.' On top of everything the 'governor' appointed by the Vestry, or committee, was against the London nurses with their hoity-toity and new-fangled ideas. Once Agnes Jones had to stand for two and a half hours, after a full day's work starting at 5 a.m., trying to talk him round. In spite of this, she wrote to Florence 'I really never despair and I am happier than I have ever been in one of the happiest lives, I suppose, anyone was ever allowed to live.'

Within three years she had 'reduced one of the most disorderly hospital populations in the world,' Florence wrote, 'to something like Christian discipline'. Moreover she had won over the Vestry by the unexpected fact that it was costing less, not more, to maintain sick paupers under her regime. 'She had disarmed all opposition, all sectarian zealotism . . . and aged paupers made verses to her honour after her death.' Death came to her early in 1868, at the age of thirty-six, from typhus fever caught in the wards.

This was a bitter blow to Florence, who had meanwhile started a campaign to spread the Liverpool system to the rest of the country. Those reforms would need an Act of Parliament for their enforcement. Their main principle was to separate sick, insane, incurable and above all child paupers from each other instead of 'heaping up' the lot together, and to levy a general hospital rate.

Sir Harry Verney: as MP for Buckinghamshire he was able to lobby interest in Parliament for Florence's reforms. A caricature by C. Pellegrini for *Vanity Fair*.

The President of the Poor Law Board, Charles Villiers, liked the scheme, and committed himself to pressing for a new Poor Law Bill for London. Sir Harry Verney, known to some as 'the Member of Parliament for Miss Nightingale', was set to work lobbying in the Commons; Delane, editor of *The Times*, gave his support. A Metro-politan Workhouse Infirmary Bill was drafted and seemed certain to go through Parliament. Then, once again, politics upset the apple-cart. In June 1866 the Whigs went out – Charles Villiers was a Whig – and there was a new Minister in charge of Poor Law affairs, Mr Gathorne Hardy. The Bill was buried. 'It was a cruel disappointment to me,' Florence wrote, 'to see the Bill go just as I had it in my grasp.'

Gathorne Hardy was polite but aloof and did not meet her, ask her advice or answer her letters. But he did appoint a committee to report on the 'requisite amount of space, and other matters, in relation to work-houses and workhouse infirmaries'. This gave Florence an opening, small as it was. Nursing was plainly one of the 'other matters' and she sent the committee a paper on 'the system or no system reigning here' and specified the changes she thought should be made. Gathorne Hardy kept his counsel and his distance; South Street was never to become a Little Poor Law Board. But early in 1867, to Florence's surprise, he introduced a Bill to make changes in the administration of workhouse infirmaries. It did not, in her view, go nearly far enough; she dismissed it as 'a humbug', and tried to get it recast. She failed, and the Bill became law in March 1867.

MY LORD KNOWET THAT THE CHILDREN ARE TENDER

Half a loaf, to Florence, was never better than no bread. But her less exacting friends took a brighter view. Embedded in the half-loaf were several relatively minor yet none the less significant improvements. Even Florence admitted: 'This is a beginning; we shall get what we want in time.' And she did.

'It used to be said that people gave their *blood* to their country. Now they give their *ink*,' she wrote. Few people in history can have given more ink than Florence. During that summer of 1867 – she took no holiday – she was busy not only with workhouse reform, public health in India and reorganizing the India Office, but with a two-man enquiry (herself and Dr Sutherland) into the incidence of deaths in childbirth from puerperal fever. At the outset she was shocked to find an absence of statistics. Letters went out in droves to doctors, matrons, health officials, hospital authorities and sanitary engineers. The replies, tabulated and analysed, revealed a startling fact: the death-rate of women in childbirth was several times higher in hospitals and institutions generally, than among women delivered in their own homes, however poor and dirty those homes might be. In one hospital, when eight beds were crowded

The Princess Mary ward of the East London Hospital for Children in 1878. Florence's proposals for the care of mothers and their children were revolutionary in their time.

into one room, the mortality was eight per thousand; when the beds per room were halved, so was the mortality. In a big general hospital in Paris, mortality reached the alarming figure of 193 per thousand; in two small wooden-hutted hospitals for lying-in cases only in Essex, no deaths from puerperal fever had occurred at all. Although Florence could not have known why, she correctly reasoned that the safest place for women to have their babies was either at home or in small hospitals built especially for the purpose. 'Not a single lying-in woman', she wrote, 'should ever pass the doors of a general hospital.'

This enquiry occupied three years, and the results were published in 1871 as *Introductory Notes on Lying-in Institutions*, which she dedicated to 'the shade of Socrates' mother'. Douglas Galton's department at the War Office was prevailed upon to design 'a perfectly healthy and successful Lying-in Cottage, by means of great *sub-division* and incessant cleanliness and ventilation which includes the not having *any* ward *constantly* occupied'. In one such hut, six hundred lyings-in took place without a single case of puerperal fever or casualty of any kind.

Despite these mountains of labour, these rivers of ink, Florence kept in close and constant touch with the Nightingale School of Nurses and its pupils. To find trainees of the right calibre remained its greatest difficulty. Florence laid down two principles: nurses should not do the work of 'scrubbers', and no nurse was fit to become a Superintendent and train others unless she had herself gone through the training. She wanted more Agnes Joneses and they were very few and far between. Yet women were demanding the right to enter the medical profession. Why try to become doctors, she argued, when there were plenty already but such a crying demand for nurses? To her the need was everything and theories such as sex equality were naught. She was not against 'rights for women' as such. When asked to support the Women's Suffrage movement in 1867 she replied: 'that women should have the suffrage I think no one can be more deeply convinced than I. . . . But it will be years before you obtain the suffrage for women. And in the meantime there are evils which press much more hardly on women than the want of the suffrage. . . . Till a married woman can be in possession of her own property there can be no love or justice.'

'We are your Soldiers, and we look for the approval of our Chief,' Agnes Jones had written to the revered Miss Nightingale. It was in this spirit that graduates of the School at St Thomas' came in batches to South Street to receive their Chief's blessing before taking up positions on their chosen battlefields. They might be going only as far as Highgate, where the first hospital to be built under the Workhouse Infirmary Act of 1867 was opening with a staff of nine Nightingale Nurses under an outstanding matron, Elizabeth Torrance; or they might be going to New South Wales, under Lucy Osburn, who with her band of five trained nurses found the Sydney Infirmary to be in almost as deplorable a state as the Workhouse Infirmary in Liverpool. Wherever they were posted, the Superintendents kept up a copious correspondence with their Chief – Miss Torrance's letters averaged two a week – and the Chief answered. She was by now all but deified. After their visit, one batch of

The new St Pancras Infirmary, Highgate: Elizabeth Torrance, a former pupil at the Nightingale School, became its first matron.

nurses, wrote Mrs Wardroper, was 'overflowing with love and gratitude. . . . Your reception, your pretty presents and good advice have
quite won their hearts.' 'That I have seen Miss Nightingale will be one
of the white milestones on my road,' recorded one of them. Long before
the practice was named and its techniques invented, there was little
Florence did not know about the art of public relations.

In 1868 Lord Mayo was appointed to succeed Sir John Lawrence and
wrote to South Street asking for an interview. A memorandum was soon
in his hands – 'a noble and most complete Paper', according to Sir
Bartle Frere. Florence had widened her range. Proper drainage, sewerage,
ventilation, water supplies were not enough to keep the Indians healthy
unless they were also properly fed. Nine Indians out of ten were either
actually hungry or else so badly nourished that they fell an easy prey to
disease. So 'sanitary matters' must include food, which meant that the
whole of agriculture must be radically changed. The key to this, she
saw, lay in irrigation. It now became her duty to impress on every
available servant of the Raj his duty to put irrigation at the top of his
priorities. Lord Mayo was receptive: 'the most open man, except Sidney
Herbert, I ever knew'. So was Lord Napier, now Governor of Madras
and busy spreading her doctrines all over that Province – better jails, a
hospital for women, women nurses in the wards, improved wells and
many irrigation canals. '*You* shall have the little labour that is left in
me,' he told her in 1869.

Then came another Lord Napier, the hero of Magdala, shortly to be
appointed Commander-in-Chief. He called on her in December 1869
and found an immediate place in her pantheon. She 'loved with all my
mind and heart' Lord Lawrence and Sir Bartle Frere, and now Lord
Napier of Magdala made up a trinity. There was not a Minister in
England since Sidney Herbert fit to tie their shoes. The following year
Lord Napier paid a second visit. 'He actually spent his last morning in
England with me, starting from this house. And I sent away the CIC
to India without anything to eat! He said he had too much to talk about
to waste his time in eating.' Their ideas fitted like mortice and tennon;
he was resolved to improve the soldiers' lot by providing good living
conditions and means of recreation. No wonder Jowett called her 'the

Governess of the Governors of India', to which she retorted that 'Maid of all (Dirty) Work' would be more appropriate. Lesser fry – sanitary commissioners, municipal engineers and the like – also came to be lectured, advised and probed. Indians came too. 'I have been quite beset by Parsees,' she wrote. One of them talked philosophy while she was trying to concentrate on midwifery. She wrote a pamphlet addressed to village elders telling them what simple measures they should take to improve the peasants' health and reduce mortality.

So, from her sofa in Mayfair, surrounded by cats and Mr Rathbone's flowers, she exercised a close, continuous and detailed influence over the affairs of a sub-continent she had never seen. There were dissidents, of course. John Strachey, member of the Viceroy's Council, wrote a fierce rebuttal of a memorandum drawn up by Sir Bartle Frere – 'the nastiest pill we have had', Florence remarked, adding, 'but we have swallowed a good many and we're not poisoned yet'. But it was Strachey who subsequently said: 'Of the sanitary improvements in India three-fourths are due to Miss Nightingale.'

Throughout these years of unremitting toil, she scarcely had a day free from headaches, nausea and attacks of breathlessness. Several complete breakdowns forced her to retreat to Malvern, where Dr Walter Johnson did his best to restore her. One came at the end of 1867 when she 'fled to Malvern with a small cat'. She was back in a month, but after this was never able to work in London for a long unbroken stretch, and in 1868, on the insistence of Jowett on whom she was coming more and more to rely, spent three months at Lea Hurst with her mother. Fanny was now eighty, feeble and blind. Bygones were bygones, and after 1868 Florence spent three months of each year at Embley or at Lea Hurst. Not that she was idle. At Jowett's suggestion she embarked on a treatise on the reform of the Poor Law, which she boiled down to an article published in *Fraser's Magazine* in March 1869 and called *A Note on Pauperism*. In it she supported emigration, to bring 'the landless man to the manless lands'. A large correspondence followed. In former years the facts she gathered would probably have become a book with a long, unwieldy title and a great array of statistics. But, at forty-eight, she was no longer able to drive herself so ruthlessly, and the notes were laid aside.

The outbreak of the Franco-Prussian War plunged her into another stream of work. In July 1870 the National Society for Aid to the Sick and Wounded, precursor of the British Red Cross, was formed with her blessing. From all over the world contributions poured in, and many were sent direct to her in the belief that wherever there were sick and wounded, there she would be. She was touched to receive 'sums collected by halfpence from poor hardworking negro congregations in different islands of the West Indies. . . . Puritan chapels in my own dear hills, National Schools, Factories. . . .' Authorities on both sides wrote for her advice on the design and operation of wartime hospitals. 'Every man and woman in the world seems to have come into it with the express purpose of writing to me,' she complained to Mary Mohl. 'Would I could go to the seat of War instead of all this writing, writing, writing.' But out of it all one more movement came into being. The founder of the Red Cross and of the Geneva Convention, Jean Henri Dunant, said in 1872: 'It is to an Englishwoman that all the honour of that Convention is due. What inspired me . . . was the work of Miss Florence Nightingale in the Crimea.' And as a result of her friendship with the Crown Princess of Prussia, the Victoria School of Nurses was established in Berlin on the model of the Nightingale School, and Victoria Sisters became the German counterparts of Nightingale Nurses. Her influence was spreading throughout the world.

At the start of 1872 Florence wrote: 'This year I go out of office.' The struggle with officialdom, the unrelenting effort to influence policy and get things done, were ending. She had been hard at it for eighteen years. When, early in 1872, a new Viceroy went to India without calling on her before he left, she believed that her power to influence the Government of India was over.

Yet idleness was inconceivable. 'Now in old age I never wish to be relieved from new work, but only to have it to do.' She focused her attention on the Nightingale School, enlarged after the opening of the new St Thomas' in June 1871. The School, she said, must also be 'a Home – a place of moral, religious and practical training'. A Home Sister was appointed to befriend the probationers and encourage them to read, attend Bible classes, listen to music and broaden their interests.

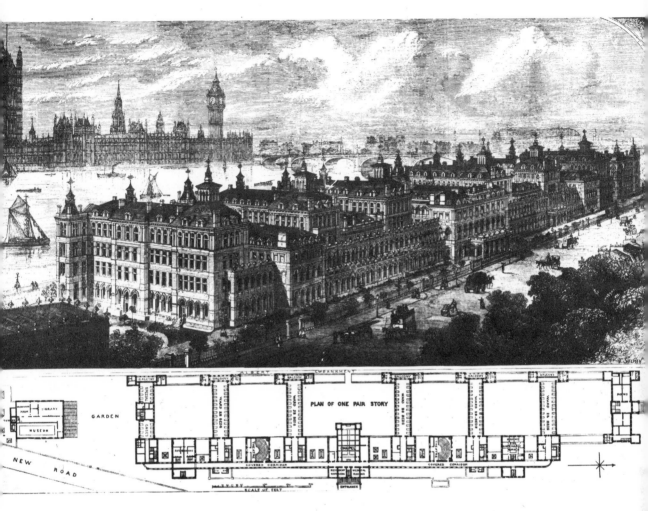

With one of the surgeons she drew up their examination papers and, when each probationer left, wrote her own assessment of the young woman's character. 'Tittupy, flippant, pretension-y, veil down, ambi-tious, clever, not much feeling, talky, underbred, no religion, may be persevering from ambition to excel, but takes things up as an adventure like Nap III.' 'As self-comfortable a jackass (or Joanass) as ever I saw.' 'A woman of good feeling and bad sense; much under the meridian of anyone who will try to persuade her. . . . Such long-winded stories five points or at least half the compass off the subject in hand.' 'As poor a two-fisted thing as ever I saw, a mawkin to frighten away good nurses.'

The new buildings of St Thomas' Hospital which were opened in June 1871, with a plan of the interior.

Sometimes, after the interview she held with each departing nurse, she wrote a little homily. 'Forgive me, dear Miss x, do you think you have the true *love* of the *best* in nursing? This is a question I ask myself daily in all I do. Do not think me governess-ing. It is a question which each one of us can only ask of, and answer to, herself.' To say that she kept her finger on the pulse of her Training School would be an under-statement. Almost did she become the artery that caused the pulse to beat.

A nurse returning to the north found a luncheon-basket waiting in her railway carriage; another, who had been ill, received a diet sheet with the note: 'Get the things out of my money.' Run-down nurses were invited to convalesce at Embley or Lea Hurst, and sometimes to South Street for a weekend in bed. Each probationer was invited, by herself, to tea, and given a present, often a cake. One of the young women, dressed in her best to obey the summons, heard at the last moment that the poverty of the guest's attire determined the size of the cake. Hastily changing into her oldest clothes, she returned from the tea-party with a cake large enough to feed all thirty-six probationers.

On taking up her first post, every nurse found flowers in her room with an affectionate message. She soon found, also, that the Chief's eye was on her wherever she might be. Florence kept up a constantly widening correspondence with all the matrons, and many of the sisters, from the Nightingale School. Over a hundred letters written by her to one matron in one year were no exception. In return, she expected from her disciples absolute loyalty, devotion to their profession, diligence and moral standards beyond reproach. The devotion she had lavished on her Master she now transferred to certain of the young graduates of her School. Angelique Pringle, a small, attractive young woman and an outstanding nurse, was addressed by Florence sometimes as 'the Pearl', sometimes as 'Little Sister', and once, when Miss Pringle left South Street without eating her dinner and Florence sent it after her in a cab, as 'Extraordinary Little Villainess'. 'Dearest, very dearest,' Florence wrote, 'Very precious to me is your note. . . . Make up your dear mind to a long holiday: that's what you have to do now. God bless you.' In return Florence was addressed as 'My own Mother-in-Chief' and 'Honoured Chief', and told 'I am so glad to be your child, and go where you want me.' Florence wanted her to go to the Edinburgh Royal Infirmary, and there she went; later she took over at St Thomas's from Mrs Wardroper.

Then there was Rachel Williams, a strikingly handsome woman Florence likened to a goddess, and called 'the Goddess-baby', since she had a petulant side. She, too, received fulsome letters from the Honoured Chief. 'I am well aware that my dear Goddess-baby has – well, a baby-side, I shall not be surprised at any outburst. . . . Don't break yourself down, dear child. . . .' 'I have this moment received your charming letter, which is just like yourself. And I *must* write and thank you for it at once. . . . It is a pure joy to me. . . . And life has not many joys for me, my darling.' In time there was scarcely an important hospital in Britain without a Nightingale Nurse as matron, and many outside Britain as well. 'I am immersed in such a torrent of my trained matrons and nurses, going and coming,' Florence wrote in June 1873, 'to and from Edin-burgh and Dublin, to and from watering-places for their health, dining, tea-ing, sleeping – sleeping by day as well as by night.'

In January 1874 Florence's father died. Her mother at eighty-six was entering second childhood. All the property went to Mr Nightingale's nephew Shore Smith, and Embley had to be given up. Bedridden and resentful, Florence had to take charge. She found herself immersed in the tiresome and boring business of sacking and engaging staff, transferring a bewildered mother to Lea Hurst, and all the minutiae of domestic detail. She was losing all her friends. Selina Bracebridge died, and her grief was heart-rending. They had always spent the anniversary of Sidney Herbert's death together. Julius Mohl died. At Lea Hurst she was shut off from the world with an imbecile mother, quarrelling servants and an overpowering sense of frustration. 'Oh God, let me not sink in these perplexities; but give me a great cause to do and die for.' No cause came. One night she noticed a shadow cast by the night-light on the wall and thought of Scutari. 'Am I she who once stood on that Crimean height? "The Lady with a Lamp shall stand." The lamp shows me only my utter shipwreck.'

In this predicament her thoughts turned again to questions of religion and the purposes of man. 'During the ten years and more that I have known you,' Jowett wrote in 1872, 'you have repeated to me the expression "Character of God" about a thousand times, but I can't say I have any clear idea of what you mean.' He suggested that she should concentrate her thoughts into several short essays. 'You will do a good work if you point out the kind of mysticism which is needed in the present day – not mysticism at all, but as intense a feeling as the mystics had of the power of truth and reason and of the will of God. . . .' She wrote three essays on this topic, two of which appeared in *Fraser's Magazine* in 1873. She was also helping Jowett with a new translation of Plato, and sending him suggestions for sermons which he worked up and preached at Oxford. At the same time she was trying to clarify her own responses to the writings of the Christian mystics, and her view of man's relationship with God.

'Religion is not devotion, but work and suffering for the love of God: this is the true doctrine of Mystics,' she wrote. 'Where shall I find God? In myself. That is the true Mystical Doctrine. But then I myself must be in a state for Him to come and dwell in me. That is the whole aim of the Mystical Life.' That she had failed in this now became a source of spiritual torment. 'True religion is to have no other will but God's,' she quoted from a sixteenth-century work. She had failed to subjugate her will to God's. She had failed in so many other ways. 'Everything has gone from my life except pain.' She had been head-strong, self-willed, had tried to force her will on God rather than to seek God's will for her. She covered scraps of paper with self-communings through whose gloom shot occasional shafts of her particular humour: 'I *must* remember God is not my private secretary.' Another, presumably referring to a cat, ran: 'O Lord I offer him to Thee. He is so *heavy*. Do Thou take care of him. *I* can't.' As the years of her mother's senility dragged on, the notes accumulated, but the work, to be called *Notes from Devotional Authors of the Middle Ages, Collected, Chosen and Freely translated by Florence Nightingale*, was never completed.

At the time of Scutari many verses had been written about 'the Lady with a Lamp'. One, by an American Baptist, she came across years later and found 'exactly true'. It ran:

> I ask no heaven till earth be Thine,
> Nor glory-crown, while work of mine

Remaineth here. When earth shall shine
　　Among the stars,
Her sins wiped out, her captives free,
Her voice a music unto Thee,
For Crown, New Work give Thou to me.
　　Lord here am I.

'Wretch that I was,' she wrote nearly twenty years later, 'not to see that God was taking from me all human help in order to compel me to lean on Him alone.'

Despite her preoccupation with religion, her enslavement to her sick mother and her isolation from the world, she had by no means abandoned her interest in Indian affairs. She continued to correspond with Indian authorities and to press on Cabinet Ministers the urgent need for reform. The drains of Madras continued to engage her attention. (During their correspondence Lord Salisbury, back from a conference in the Turkish capital, could not resist telling her: 'I was much impressed at Constantinople with the advantage of having no drains at all, but keeping dogs instead.') The miseries of Indian famine and chronic starvation continued to haunt her mind, and her campaign for irrigation took on new force when she got in touch with Sir Arthur Cotton, the leading irrigationist of the day, who wrote to her: 'If fifty years of hard work and contempt [from the Indian Government] had produced no other return but a letter from you, it would be an honour beyond what I deserve.' In 1874 her pamphlet *Life or Death in India* attracted attention and in 1878 an article in the *Nineteenth Century* tried to jolt British readers out of their complacency. In that same year the death of Lord Lawrence moved her deeply: 'O that I could do something for India for which he lived and died!' She eulogized him – 'the simplicity, the unselfishness, the firmness'; his rectitude and his physical beauty. His widow wished to give her a personal memento, but all his possessions consisted of some patched boots, a twenty-year-old watch and a walking-stick; his secretary had his old shoe-horn.

Florence was planning a book to be called *The Zemindar, the Sun and the Watering Pot as Affecting Life or Death in India*, and completed a first draft in 1874, but Jowett objected to its 'faults of taste and exaggeration'.

She took his criticisms to heart and worked on the book intermittently for the next five or six years, but never finished it.

'Do you know what have been the hardest years of my life?' she wrote to Mary Mohl in 1879. 'Not the Crimean War. Not the five years with Sidney Herbert when I sometimes worked twenty-two hours a day. But the last five years and three-quarters since my father's death.' In February 1880 – Florence was by then almost sixty – Fanny died at the age of ninety-two. To Queen Victoria's letter of condolence, Florence replied by asking permission to address the Sovereign on the sufferings of the Indian people. Permission was granted, and a memorandum followed in a few days. The Queen made no reply, but sent Florence a copy of *The Life of the Prince Consort*.

After a nervous collapse, Florence's life settled into a routine which lasted for most of her remaining years. It was a strict and orderly but very comfortable routine. She was well served. For many years she had a personal maid called Temperance Thatcher who married the Russian orphan she had brought back from the Crimea and installed as a footman at Embley. She kept a commissionaire who carried her numerous messages all over London, and a female staff of five.

She was a small but fastidious eater, and kept as close a watch on the kitchen as on other matters. A menu would be drawn up every day and next morning the cook received her comments, some predictably caustic. 'Meat hard, and remember that mincing makes hard meat harder.' For Rachel Williams she would order special dishes: 'Rissoles, or fillets of sole à la Maître d'hôtel, or oyster patties, or omelette aux fines herbes, or chicken à la mayonnaise with aspic jelly.' Cakes, coffee and fresh eggs she sent regularly to St Thomas'; soufflés and jellies were dispatched to several invalids in the north.

Her guests were positively pampered. First came morning tea, then a visit from Temperance Thatcher to enquire how the guest had slept; and what about plans for the day? Had the visitor any friends she would like asked to luncheon? Then an appointment with the Chief, and possibly a visit to the Verneys who lived a few doors away. Or Parthe might take the guest for a drive, or Sir Harry take her to the House of Commons to hear a debate. The big moment of the day was the interview with the

OPPOSITE Claydon House, the home of the Verneys. Florence was to spend more and more time there. She formed close bonds with members of the Verney family, particularly after Parthe's death.

Chief. 'At times Miss Nightingale was well enough to come down to the drawing-room and rest on a couch there while she received her guests,' one of her former pupils recalled. 'Her couch or bed was always strewn with letters and papers, and a pencil was ever at hand. She was dressed in soft black silk with a shawl over her feet; always the transparent white kerchief laid over her hair and tied under the chin.'

Persian kittens were sometimes around. A constant flow of notes passed to and fro; even her closest relatives and friends might see her only by appointment. With some pathos, one of these, Lady Ashburton, wrote: 'I wish that you would let me sit like a poor old rat in the corner, while you are at dinner; it is much wholesomer not to eat in solitude but I know I shan't get in, so I can only leave this at the door.' In a postscript Lady Ashburton's daughter asked 'with her dear love if you could see her any time today; she will talk through the keyhole and not detain you five minutes.' Bedroom and drawing-room were light, airy, full of flowers, simply but neatly furnished; book-cases were to be found all over the house. In the dining-room, the shelves were filled with blue books with the sole exception of *The Ring and the Book*.

'Stranger vicissitudes than mine in life few men have had – vicissitudes from slavery to power, and from power to slavery again,' Florence had written to Mary Mohl. Now a new vicissitude brought back some of the power. Her old friend Lord de Grey, now Lord Ripon, became Viceroy. He was a reformer, and was going to be the saviour of India; it looked as if a new day had dawned. From South Street a stream of notes, digests and proposals flowed out to Delhi. 'How well you know the subject of Indian sanitation,' Lord Ripon responded in 1883; and no less well those of land reform, usury and peasant agriculture.

Lord Ripon's reforms were fought tooth and nail by the old guard in India and at the India Office, and Florence constituted herself Lord Ripon's public relations officer. Once more she built up a network of influential contacts; once more Governors came to call before taking up their appointments and so did Lord Roberts, the new Commander-in-Chief in 1881. She wrote a paper for the East India Association, read at Exeter Hall in June 1883, in defence of Lord Ripon's Bengal Land Tenure Bill which had run into trouble – she out-Nightingaled herself in

OPPOSITE Florence in her old age, painted by Richardson. The reforming firebrand of former years, who would pester ministers until she had her way, became gentler as the years passed. This portrait now hangs at Claydon House.

Florence, watching at the window, joins a group of Nightingale nurses photographed at Claydon in 1887. Her warm relationships with her nurses made her old age a happy one. In the picture also are Sir Harry Verney and Parthe (extreme left).

titling it *The Dumb Shall Speak, and the Deaf Shall Hear, or, the Ryot, the Zemindar and the Government.* A scheme was introduced to allow candi-dates for the Indian Civil Service a year's study at the University before going to their posts. She suggested in some detail a course in 'the peculiar wants of India' – agricultural chemistry and botany, geology, forestry and animal physiology. 'What if Scientific Agriculture could be taught at Oxford?' – a revolutionary thought in 1882. In due course it was. She even found a lecturer, an old friend Sir George Campbell.

In Egypt, British forces under Lord Wolseley were engaged in a campaign. Nurses were called for, and Florence was invited to help in their selection. 'I have been working some days from 4.30 a.m. till 10 p.m.,' she reported in August 1882. One of her trained matrons, Mrs Deebles, was put in charge of a party of twenty-four. The following November 'for the first time for twenty-five years, I went out to see a sight' – to Victoria Station to see the return of the Foot Guards from Egypt. The men were like shabby skeletons, but their uniforms were clean and tidy; they were 'alert, silent, steady'. Her 'children' had not changed. Now that the ban on going out was lifted, Florence was enticed forth again: to a Royal Review of the returned campaigners, where she sat between Mr and Mrs Gladstone, and to the opening of the new Law Courts by the Queen in December 1882.

The Egyptian campaign brought to light defects in the army's medical and hospital organization. 'It is the Crimea over again,' Florence exclaimed. It was not quite as bad as that, but letters from Mrs Deebles and her nurses supplied her with disquieting facts, and when a com-mittee of enquiry was set up, she was ready, as in former days, to suggest witnesses, supply the right questions to ask them, read the daily minutes sent to her by a friend on the committee, Lord Wantage, and write papers to be incorporated into the report. 'I am bound to say', Lord Wantage wrote, 'that many of the best suggestions come from you, and for these I beg to thank you most sincerely.'

In 1883 the Queen conferred the Royal Red Cross upon her for her 'special exertions in providing for the nursing of the sick and wounded soldiers and sailors'. She took the opportunity to write two long letters to the Queen, one on the state of the army medical services and the other

ABOVE Mrs Deebles, of the Army Nursing Service, who supervised the party of nurses sent to Egypt in 1882. This illustration, published in 1879, shows her with a group of nurses who accompanied her to Natal.

To report at outposts *en route.* 25.   All Vehicles to be searched.

PA SS.

The bearer...*Nursing Sister Latham*

has permission to proceed to...*a fro through outposts*

per...*Anyhow*

Time allowed...*Permanent*

Kroonstad,   *AA Chichester*
                                                        Capt.,
Date...........................   Assistant Provost Marshal,

LEFT An army pass issued to a nurse during the Boer War. Nursing staff in foreign postings inevitably came under military jurisdiction.

enlisting support for Lord Ripon's Indian reforms. But shortly afterwards the opposition proved too much for him and he suddenly resigned.
Florence accused him of 'deserting the Empire' but his successor, Lord
Dufferin, kept up the tradition of calling on Miss Nightingale for a
briefing. He was the fifth Viceroy to observe it. Lord Dufferin proved
regrettably ignorant about 'Indian sanitary things', but said: 'Give me
your instructions and I will carry them out. Supply the powder and I
will fire the shot.' It seemed that now, at the age of sixty-four, she was
back 'in office' again.

There was a difference: she who had always given orders must now
ask for orders herself. An urgent appeal went out to Dr Sutherland:
'Give me quickly what instructions you think I should send him.' This
was on a Friday; the notes must reach her before Monday. Dr Sutherland
rebelled. He was busy looking at the cholera baccillus 'with a beautiful
Vienna microscope' and so 'the Viceroy must wait.' This was intolerable;
notes and telegrams sped from Mayfair to Norwood. 'I did not know the
baccillus was of more consequence than a Viceroy.' Dr Sutherland
stood firm: Dr Koch and his cholera baccillus, he said, would save many
more lives than Lord Dufferin could hope to do. Luckily Lord Dufferin's departure was postponed for a few days and he was able to take
with him to beguile the voyage a formidable dossier of Notes.

General Gordon was another caller who became a devotee; their
views on work, God and duty were much the same. In 1884 he was
besieged in Khartoum, and a party of women nurses was ordered to
Wadi Halfa as part of the Relief Expedition. Florence was elated. 'It is
thirty-four years since I was at Wadi Halfa. How little could I ever have
thought that there would be trained nurses there now! O faithless me,
that think God cannot make His firmament without pillars.' The
superintendent of the party was her former 'Goddess-baby', Rachel
Williams. One of its members, Phillippa Hicks, was on duty at King's
College Hospital on a Saturday morning when Miss Nightingale's
commissionaire arrived with a note. Would Sister Hicks leave in three
days' time for the Sudan? If so, she was to report at South Street for
instructions at 8.30 a.m. on the following Monday.

There the 'warm-hearted old lady' mingled her practical hints with

General Gordon, in Indian dress. His integrity in dealing with indigenous peoples provoked the hostility of many British Government officials. Of them he said: 'To me they are utterly wrong in the government of the subject races, they know nothing of the hearts of these people, and oil and water would as soon mix as the two races.' In England he spent much time working with the underprivileged and after his death a Gordon Home for Destitute Boys was set up in his memory.

injunctions to 'see that your every word and act is worthy of your pro-fession and your woman-hood'. As a parting present Miss Hicks received a folding rubber bath. When the nurses got on board their ship at Tilbury, each one found a bouquet of flowers in her cabin with the message 'God-speed from Florence Nightingale'. On their return Phillippa Hicks found number 10, South Street and its staff at her disposal and was invited to Claydon for a month. During the nurses' brief absence, February to August 1885, Florence wrote sixty-five letters to Rachel Williams – an average of considerably better than two a week. ('Would that I could help you to nurse the Typhoids! . . . Cheer up, fight the good fight of faith.')

Richard Monckton Milnes in 1870: a watercolour by C. Pellegrini, contributed to *Vanity Fair*. The loss of the man whom she had once loved and who had encouraged her throughout her life weighed heavily on her.

The success of the Wadi Halfa expedition was a bright ray in a life that had become sombre in its hue. Her health remained precarious, she slept badly and she was often overcome by a conviction of her own inadequacy and failure. Dr Jowett urged her frequently to dwell more on the bright side: on what she had achieved, not on her relative failures. 'Everybody has heard of you and has a sweet association with your name.' But self-reproach had always come more easily to her than self-gratification; the saying *Horas non numero nisi serenas* [I don't count the hours unless they have been happy] did not apply to her. She was paying, too, the penalty of longevity; all her old friends were going. In 1882 Dr Farr died. Then in 1883 in a single month, May, came two dreadful losses: her oldest surviving friend, Mary Mohl, and her coun-sellor and *guru*, Sir John McNeill. The following year carried off Sir Bartle Frere, and the year after that her old flame Richard Monckton Milnes, by then Lord Houghton. She felt old, unworthy, lonely. On Christmas Day 1885 she wrote: 'Let me dedicate this poor old crumbling woman to Thee. Behold the handmaid of the Lord. I was Thy hand-maid as a girl. Now I have back-slidden!'

In 1888 Dr Sutherland resigned from his position on the Army Sanitary Commission, on which he had toiled for so many years. He was nearly eighty – too old for digging ponds, even for studying baccilli. He had given his whole life to two linked causes: the health of the British army, and Florence Nightingale. Only three years of retirement were left to him. 'Give her my love and blessing,' were said to be Dr Sutherland's last words to his wife when, in 1891, he passed from the scene.

Though by then over seventy and lost without Dr Sutherland, this indefatigable woman soldiered on in the cause of Indian public health. In 1891 an International Congress of Hygiene and Demography was held in London with Douglas Galton in charge. Florence saw to it that an Indian section was formed, and stirred up the Indians themselves to send delegates. Sir Harry Verney was persuaded to invite them to Claydon in batches and there Florence arranged to see them 'one by one'. The Bombay Village Sanitation Act was bogged down in financial difficulties, and Florence canvassed for signatures to a set of proposals which she sent to the Secretary of State, the Viceroy and the Governor of Bombay. Articles on Health Lectures for Indian Villages (1893), Village Sanitation in India (1894) and Heath Missionaries for Rural India (1896) followed. Very little came of all this activity. 'You have most effectively drawn attention to the subject,' one of her friends wrote, and this summed up the limit of her powers.

For years her sister Parthe had been crippled with arthritis, and in May 1890 she died. Sir Harry Verney was nearly ninety and his affection for his sister-in-law had grown and deepened with the years. Now she went increasingly to Claydon to keep him company and help to manage his affairs. In the course of doing so, she made a remarkable discovery, somewhat late in the day. This was that the villages of Buckinghamshire were almost, if not quite, as badly in need of sanitary reform as the villages of India. Sir Harry's son, Frederick Verney, was enlisted, and in a very short while she had the local Health Officer holding classes and arranging tours of villages for ladies to be enrolled as Health Missionaries, a new order she brought into being in 1892.

All this time she kept up an enormous correspondence, not only on business, but with old friends and a host of relations, young and old. Her genius for friendship is attested by the many letters she received from people of all kinds. Colonel Yule, whom she had met on the India Council, dictated from his deathbed: 'I praise God for the privilege of having known you.' Mr Croft, who for many years instructed the probationers at St Thomas', wrote of 'so lovable and adorable a leader as Miss Nightingale'. Her own letters dealt with an enormous range of

topics: the behaviour of a snail brought in on a tulip, her opinion of the Ghost in Hamlet, the cooking of Egyptian lentils, Villari's *Savonarola*, facets of her own philosophy.

I learn the lesson of life from a little kitten of mine, one of two. The old cat comes in and says, very cross, 'I didn't ask you in here, I like to have my Missus to myself!' And he runs at them. The bigger and handsomer kitten runs away, but the littler one *stands her ground*, and when the old enemy comes near enough kisses his nose, and makes the peace. That is the lesson of life, to kiss one's enemy's nose, always standing one's ground.

She had always stood her ground and stood it now until her senses failed her. In twelve months, 1893–4, the three remaining people she loved most were taken from her: Sir Harry Verney, her cousin Shore Smith and Benjamin Jowett. The longer Jowett had known her, the deeper had his affection grown. It became devotion. When he was taken ill in Oxford, telegrams and letters went to her daily to report on his condition. He recovered, but collapsed again the following year. A fortnight before his death, he dictated a farewell letter: 'How greatly am I indebted to you for all your affection. How large a part has your life been of my life. There is only time I think for a few words.' He died in October 1893.

Twenty years earlier, she would have railed at fate or been crushed by the bereavement; she was calmer now. 'I have lost much in failures and disappointment, as well as in grief; but do you know, life is more precious to me now in my old age.' Her mind's cutting edge was beginning to be blunted. She pondered more, dozed more, fretted less, was more easily pleased. Gentleness and benevolence replaced the acerbities of former years. Even her appearance softened. She who had been so lithe and slim and eager grew round and full in the face, matronly, slow in her movements. Jowett had told her that the last years of life were the happiest and, with her, so it proved. Not that she gave way to idleness. In 1897 she thanked God, she wrote, for giving her 'work, constant work, work with Sidney Herbert, work with Lord Lawrence, and never out of work still'. In 1898 she was sufficiently alert to engage in a long discussion with the Aga Khan, in which she outlined the material advances she had seen in her lifetime. 'Do you think you are improving?'

OPPOSITE The Blue Room at Claydon House, as it was in Florence's time.

he asked. By improving he meant 'Believing more in God'. Regretfully, she noted: 'A most interesting man, but you could never teach him sanitation.' In 1896 the barracks at Hong Kong drew forth a memorandum for the Secretary of War and the Colonial Secretary. It was not until 1906, when she was eighty-six, that the India Office was informed that she could no longer usefully be sent Sanitary Papers for her perusal.

A proposal to stage an exhibit about the progress of nursing as part of the Diamond Jubilee celebrations drew forth a withering blast from the old lady of South Street. 'Oh, the absurdity of people, and the vulgarity! . . . I will not give my foolish Portrait (which I have not got) or anything else as 'relics' of the Crimea. It is too ridiculous. You don't judge even of the victuals inside a public-house by the sign outside. . . . And you ask me for the photograph of a rat!' But she yielded to the charm of Lady Wantage, and her bust and the 'Russian car', discovered 'all in pieces in an Embley farm-house', were put on display. To her great annoyance, flowers were seen to bedeck the bust, and an old soldier to kiss the Crimean carriage.

Her sight had been deteriorating for some years and in 1901 gave way altogether. The stream of notes that had issued from her indelible pencil ceased to flow. All her life these notes, and all her innumerable letters, had been written in a neat, clear, apparently unhurried, elegant hand. Nothing was blurred or illegible, and she used none of the squiggles writers often employ as a personal shorthand. But from about 1902 onwards her hands, for the first time in her life, lay idle at her side. For the first time also she had a secretary-companion who read to her the daily newspapers, essays and biographies. Then it was time for a nurse, who found her an amiable but difficult patient. Sometimes, when she had been tucked in for the night, she would get out of bed to go and tuck up the nurse. Sometimes she would recite passages from Milton and Shelley, and from Italian and French writers, in clear tones, and sometimes she would sing half-forgotten arias from Italian opera. She could receive few visitors, but almost to the end welcomed calls from Nightingale Nurses who remained close to her heart.

In November 1907 the King conferred upon her the Order of Merit and in December it was delivered in a cab. She was too senile to under-

Letter from Miss FLORENCE NIGHTINGALE.

Dec 16/96

10, SOUTH STREET,
PARK LANE, W.

Dear Duke of Westminster
Good speed to your
noble effort in favour of
District Nurses for town
& country; and in
commemoration of our
Queen who cares for all.
We look upon the
District Nurse, if she is
what she should be, &
if we give her the training
she should have, as the
Great civilizer of the poor.
training as well as nursing
them out of ill health
into good health (Health
Missioners), out of drink
into self control but all
without preaching, without

patronizing — as friends
in sympathy.
But let them hold the
Standard high as Nurses
Pray be sure I will try
to help all I can, tho'
that be small, here
I will with your leave
let you know.
Pray believe me
your Grace's faithful
servant
Florence Nightingale

A letter addressed to the Duke of Westminster in 1896 on the subject of district nurses. It was not until ten years later that government officials were tactfully to cease consulting her opinion on nursing matters.

stand what it was all about and merely murmured 'Too kind, too kind.' Ten years earlier she would doubtless have made some much more brusque comment, if indeed she had agreed to accept the Order at all. It was the first time a woman had received it, and Lord Roberts observed that the award was an honour bestowed upon the Order of Merit.

As her mind softened, so did her memories. Among her few visitors was Miss Pringle ('the Pearl'), who found her 'sitting up by the fire in the familiar room, her mind evidently busy with happy thoughts'. Some must surely have been of Sidney Herbert, the love of her life. Richard Monckton Milnes had been forgotten, but sometimes she would ask for Sir Harry Verney. On 13 August 1910 she fell asleep and did not wake. After life's fitful fever, no one could have had a calmer end.

Burial in Westminster Abbey was proposed, but by her own choice her funeral was a very simple one. The directions in her Will were not fully carried out. She wished her remains to be used 'for dissection or post-mortem examination for the purposes of Medical Science' and then 'carried to the nearest burial ground accompanied by not more than two persons without trappings'. In the event six sergeants of the Guards bore the coffin to a grave beside those of her father and mother at East Wellow, near Embley. The churchyard was gay with flowers and packed with a great crowd of people, mostly poorly dressed. At her request her only memorial was a small cross with the letters F N and the inscription 'Born 1820. Died 1910.'

Begun in the reign of George IV and ended in that of Edward VII, her life more than spanned the whole Victorian era. 'Do you think you are improving?' had asked the Aga Khan. She would not have hesitated for an instant in her reply. Life for the majority had improved, was improving and would continue to improve. Grieved greatly by his imperfections, she still believed in the ultimate perfectability of man. Few of the great Victorians brought about by their personal efforts more of the material improvements of the era than Florence Nightingale. Probably in her own mind the betterment of the soldiers' lot, in sickness and in health, that she had helped to bring about would have rated highest. Next to that would have come her efforts to better the health of the peasants of India. Today she is remembered first and foremost as the founder of the nursing profession in its modern form. Her thirty-eight ragtag-and-bobtail women, who coped with the shambles at Scutari, and the fifteen young ladies introduced into St Thomas' in 1860, were the start of one of the greatest of all services to mankind. This was her achievement, and almost hers alone.

Like all people of genius, her nature was a mass of contradictions. At once mystic and materialist, emotional and hard-headed, generous and exacting, compassionate and ruthless, humble and over-bearing, humorous and severe, loyal to friends and so often intolerant of their failings, no one with whom she came into contact could remain indifferent to her personality. In this lay the key to the fascination she held for those whose life touched hers, men and women alike. She combined in one person so many different kinds of person: the gay, attractive young woman who could have had her pick of men; the scholar who could read fluently in the original Plato, Dante, Goethe, Molière: the music-mad debutante and the mathematician to whom statistics was the greatest science in the world; the skilful nurse; the brilliant administrator; the witty conversationalist; the seeker after truth and servant of God. Of a universal God, rather than the particular god of one or other Christian sect; dogma, creed and rite she discarded, striving towards a universal truth about the spiritual nature of man. Despite her deep and passionate capacity for friendship, and her love for, sometimes adoration of, her friends, to meet them as individuals in an after-life formed no part in her philosophy. In some aspects her beliefs were akin to those of modern humanists: 'For mankind to create the circumstances which create mankind through His Laws is "the way of God".' And again: 'The Kingdom of Heaven is within, but we must also make it so without.' God meant man to work for man's own improvement; the spiritual and the material were one. 'To be a good Nurse one must be a *good woman*, or one is truly nothing but a tinkling bell.'

As a woman she was formidable, seldom an attractive trait. Yet attractive she was beyond doubt. So many diverse men came under her spell – Milnes, Bracebridge, Herbert, Clough, Lawrence, McNeill, Jowett, Verney and the ever-patient Dr Sutherland; and also many women: Mary Mohl, Selina Bracebridge, Mai Smith, Hilary Bonham Carter, Liz Herbert, the nurses whose loyalty endured throughout their lives.

It is doubtful whether any saint has been an easy man or woman. Some have been half mad. Many have had a streak, as Florence had, of masochism. They have prayed and fasted, gone barefoot and hungry, seen visions, flagellated themselves. In the nineteenth century all this was out of fashion. Yet the impulses that drove the martyrs in their hair-shirts were still the motive force of the reformers in their frock-coats and bombazine. It is not as a Victorian saint that Florence would wish to be remembered. Jowett wrote that she was loved and respected 'not for the halo of glory which surrounded your name in the Crimea, but for the patient toil which you have endured since on behalf of everyone who is suffering or wretched'. But a saint, in her sober, duty-loving setting, perhaps is what she was.

"THE LADY WITH THE LAMP."

DEATH OF MISS FLORENCE NIGHTINGALE.

HEROINE OF THE CRIMEA.

STORY OF HER GREAT WORK FOR SUFFERING SOLDIERS.

We much regret to announce that Miss Florence Nightingale died at her residence, 10, South Street, London, somewhat unexpectedly on Saturday afternoon. The cause of death was heart failure. Two members of her family were present when she passed away.

Miss Nightingale, who celebrated her ninetieth birthday on May 13th, had been under the constant supervision of her doctor, Sir Thomas Barlow. Her hospital work during the Crimean War, which inspired Longfellow's well-known poem, "The Lady with the Lamp," and her singularly unassuming character had earned for her a place apart in the affectionate regard of the English people.

She was a member of the Order of Merit and had received the freedom of the City of London. The funeral, which will take place in the course of the next few days, will be of the quietest possible character, in accordance with her strongly expressed wish.

Florence's death was reported in *The Daily Graphic* on 15 August 1910. Behind the legend of 'the Lady with a Lamp' lay one of the most astonishing analytical minds of the nineteenth century.

BIBLIOGRAPHY

Cook, Sir Edward, *The Life of Florence Nightingale* (2 vols) (Macmillan 1913).

Cope, Zachary, *Florence Nightingale and the Doctors* (Museum 1958).

Cope, Zachary, *Six Disciples of Florence Nightingale* (Pitman 1961).

Douglas, Sir G., and Ramsay, Sir G. D. (eds.), *The Panmure Papers* (Hodder and Stoughton 1908).

Goodman, Margaret, *Experiences of an English Sister of Mercy* (Smith Elder 1862).

Kinglake, A. W., *The Invasion of the Crimea* (9 vols) (William Blackwood 1887).

Martineau, Harriet, *England and Her Soldiers* (Smith Elder 1859).

Memoir of Sir John McNeill and his second Wife Elizabeth (John Murray 1910).

Mitra, S. M., *The Life and Letters of Sir John Hall* (Longmans, Green 1911).

O'Malley, I. B., *Florence Nightingale 1820–1856* (Thornton Butterworth 1931).

O'Meara, K., *Madame Mohl. Her Salon and Friends* (R. Bentley and Son 1885).

Osborne, Rev. S. G., *Scutari and its Hospitals* (Dickenson Brothers 1855).

Poole, S. Lane, *Life of Lord Stratford de Redcliffe* (Longmans, Green 1888).

Reid, T. Wemyss, *Richard Monckton Milnes* (Cassell 1890).

Russell, W. H., *The British Expedition to the Crimea* (Routledge 1858).

Simpson, M. C. M., *Letters and Recollections of Julius and Mary Mohl* (Kegan, Paul 1887).

Soyer, A., *Soyer's Culinary Campaign* (Routledge 1857).

Stanmore, Lord, *Sidney Herbert: A Memoir* (John Murray 1906).

Taylor, F., *Eastern Hospitals and English Nurses* (Hurst and Blackett 1856).

Tulloch, Colonel, *The Crimean Commission and the Chelsea Board* (Harrison 1857).

Williams, Jane (ed.), *The Autobiography of Elizabeth Davis* (2 vols) (Hurst and Blackett 1857).

Woodham-Smith, Cecil, *Florence Nightingale* (Constable 1951).

Official Publications

Report upon the State of the Hospitals of the British Army in the Crimea and Scutari (Cmd 1885).

Report of the Commission of Enquiry into the Supplies of the British Army in the Crimea, McNeill and Tulloch Commission (Cmd 1856).

Report to the Right Hon. Lord Panmure, Minister at War, of the Proceedings of the Sanitary Commission, 1885–6 (Cmd March 1857).

Report of the Commissioners Appointed to Enquire into the Regulations affecting the Sanitary Condition of the Army etc, Royal Sanitary Commission (Cmd 1858).

The Royal Commission on the Sanitary State of the Army in India (Cmd 1863).

Works by Florence Nightingale

The Institution of Kaiserswerth on the Rhine for the Practical Training of Deaconesses (1851).

Letters from Egypt (Privately printed 1854).

Notes on Matters Affecting the Health, Efficiency and Hospital Administration of the British Army (Harrison and Sons 1858).

A Contribution to the Sanitary History of the British Army during the Late War with Russia (Harrison 1859).

Notes on Hospitals (John W. Parker 1859 and Longmans, Green 1863).

Suggestions for Thought to the Searchers after Truth among the Artizans of England (3 vols) (Eyre and Spottiswood 1860).

Notes on Nursing: What it is, and What it is Not (Harrison 1860).

Observations on the Sanitary State of the Army in India (Privately printed 1861).

Army Sanitary Administration and its Reform under the late Lord Herbert (McCorquodale 1862).

How People may Live and not Die in India (1863).

Suggestions of a System of Nursing for Hospitals in India (1856).

On Trained Nursing for the Sick Poor (The Metropolitan and National Nursing Association 1876).

Indian Letters. A Glimpse into the Agitation for Tenancy Reform. Bengal 1878–82. (Calcutta 1937).

INDEX

Aga Khan, the, 243–4, 246

Albert, Prince Consort, 129; and FN, 151, 185–6

Alexander, Dr Thomas, 154, 156, 166, 198

Alexandria, 184

Alma, battle of the (1854), 59, 63

Alton Locke (Kingsley), 194

American Civil War (1861–5), 196

Andes, 98

Andover (horse), 175

Argyll, Duke of, 131

Army Medical School, 153, 165, 172, 208

Army Sanitary Administration under the late Lord Herbert (FN), 182

Arthur, Prince, 129

Ashburton, Lady, 233

Ashley, Lord, 40

Athena (owl), 42, 58

Athens, 41–2

Balaclava: battle of (1855), 76, 77, 98, 120–4; camp at, 88; town, 88; hospitals, 89, 98, 109; FN at, *see* Nightingale, Florence, at Balaclava; Castle Hospital, 117, 124, 133; General Hospital, 117, 132, 142

Balmoral, 151

Bangalore, 200

Barrack Hospital, Scutari, *see* Scutari

Bengal Land Tenure Bill, 233–6

Berlin, 42, 184, 224

Bermondsey convent, 72, 146; nuns, 142, 143

Bermuda, 208

Birk Hall, 151

Board of General Officers, *see* Chelsea Board

Board of Supervision for the Relief of the Poor in Scotland, 110

Bombay, 203, 214–15

Bombay Village Sanitation Act, 241

Bonham Carter family, 14, 15

Bonham Carter, Hilary, 21, 195, 196, 247; letters from FN to, 29, 30; assists FN in work, 163, 183, 186; death, 210–11

Bracebridge, Charles, 34, 41, 42, 247; at Scutari, 71, 75, 76, 79, 83, 88, 103, 124; at Balaclava, 120; returns to England, 128; ill-judged lecture on army, 132

Bracebridge, Selina, 34, 41, 42, 247; at Scutari, 71, 75, 76; at Balaclava, 120; returns to England, 128; death, 227

Bridgeman, Mother, 132, 133, 140, 142

Brown, Sir George, 92

Brussels, 178, 184

Bunsen, Baron, 23, 27, 29, 40

Burlington Hotel: FN's residence at, 154, 159, 163, 166–8, 175, 199; 'Little War Office', 171, 172; leaves, 182; breakfast conferences at, 186

Butterfield, William, 184

Cadwaladyr, Elizabeth, *see* Davis, Elizabeth

Calcutta, 203, 207

Cambridge, Duke of, 131, 151

Campbell, Sir George, 236

Campbell, Thomas, 27

Canada, British expedition to, 196

Canning, Lady, 47

Carlsbad, 44

Carlyle, Thomas, 27

Cassandra (FN), 46

Castle Hospital, Balaclava, *see* Balaclava

Cavour, Camillo Benzo, 175

Chartres, 17

Chateaubriand, François René, 17, 20

Chatham, 163

Chelsea Board of Generals, 113

China, 173

Clark, Sir James, 151, 172, 192, 208

Clarke, Mary, *see* Mohl, Mary

Clarke, Mrs, 17

Clarke, Mrs (housekeeper), 75

Claydon, 240, 241

Clough, Arthur Hugh, 166, 171, 196, 197, 247; death, 195

Commission on the Commissariat, 110

Congrès de Bienfaisance, London, 182

Constantinople, 71, 98, 184

Cook, Sir Edward, 146, 187, 198, 199

Cotton, Sir Arthur, 229

Court, Elizabeth à, *see* Herbert, Elizabeth

Cranworth, Lady, 140

Crimean War (1854–6), 59, 62–147; peace, 141

Croft, Mr, 241

Cummings, Dr, 89, 99, 100

Dalhousie, Earl of, *see* Panmure, Lord

Davis, Elizabeth (*née* Cadwaladyr), 84, 117

de Grey, Lord (Lord Ripon), 196, 233, 238
Deebles, Mrs, 236
Delane, John Thadeus, 64, 218
Delhi, 233
Derby, Lord (14th Earl), 171, 198
Derby, Lord (15th Earl), *see* Stanley, Lord
Dorchester House, 211
Drake, Mrs, 81
Dublin, 113, 184
Dufferin, Lord, 238
Dumb Shall Speak and the Deaf Shall Hear, The, etc. (FN), 236
Dunant, Jean Henri, 224
Dunsany, Lady, 195

East India Association, 233
East India Company, 199
East Wellow, 246
Edinburgh, 151, 184
Edinburgh Royal Infirmary, 227
Edward VII, 244
Egypt: FN visits, 41; British expeditionary force in, 236
Elliott, Captain, 23
Embley Park, Romsey, 14–15, 20, 29, 168; FN at, 16, 23, 214, 223; given up by Nightingale family, 227
Essai de Physique Sociale (Quetelet), 186
Evans, Jane, 84, 146

Fairoaks, Winchester, 14, 20
Farr, Dr William, 163, 166, 186, 198–9, 203; death, 240
Filder, Mr, Commissary General, 113, 156
Fitzgerald, David, 117, 140, 142, 143
Fliedner, Pastor Theodor, 29, 44
Florence, 11, 117
Forester, Lady Maria, 70
Fox, Lady Caroline, 23
France: Nightingale family travels in, 17; in Crimean War, 59, 62, 64
Franco-Prussian War (1870–1), 224
Frankfurt, 40
Fraser's Magazine, 223, 228

Frere, Sir Bartle, 204, 214–15, 222, 223; death, 240

Galton, Captain Douglas, 21, 171, 209, 211; FN's correspondence with, 214, 215; at War Office, 220
Galton, Marianne, *see* Nicholson, Marianne
Gaskell, Mrs Elizabeth, 14, 55–8
Gathorne Hardy, 218
General Board of Health, 110
General Hospital, Balaclava, *see* Balaclava
General Hospital, Scutari, *see* Scutari
Geneva, 17
Geneva Convention, 224
Ghent, 42
Gibraltar, 209, 211
Gladstone, William Ewart, 182, 236
Golden Fleece, 104
Goodman, Sister Margaret, 104
Gordon, General Charles George, 238
Gridley Howe, Dr Samuel, 29
Guizot, François, 17, 27

Hall, Dr John, 92, 98, 109, 154; attitude to nurses, 92, 133, 140; hostility to FN, 117, 120, 131, 132; decorated, 143; and Royal Commission, 161
Hallam, Arthur, 27
Hampstead, 173, 182, 199
Hawes, Sir Benjamin, 151, 154, 168–71, 175
Herbert, Elizabeth (*née* à Court), 47, 59, 72, 104, 196; and FN's work in Crimean War, 70–1, 109; relations with FN, 35, 161, 175, 178, 247; memoir of husband, 182
Herbert, Sidney, 131, 153, 247; meets FN, 35; and hospital reform, 59; Secretary of State at War, 70, 71, 84, 104, 109; and FN's appointment in Crimea, 70, 71, 75; collaboration with FN, on Crimean campaign, 83, 100, 101–3, 107, 140, 141, 243, on army

medical reform, 150, 153–6, 157, 159, 161, 164, 168, 171–3; FN's correspondence with, 142–3, 168; and Royal Commission, 153, 154–6, 159, 161, 164–5; Minister of War, 172, 174, 175; illness, 171, 174–8; peerage, 175; death, 178–9; president of Nightingale Fund, 188
Hicks, Philippa, 238–40
Highgate, 164, 221
Histoire de mes idées (Quinet), 194
Holland, Queen of, 184, 209
Hong Kong, 244

India, 184, 224, 229, 233–6; FN's sanitary reforms in 198–208, 214–16, 238, 241; Sanitary Commission on, 198–201
India Council, 214
India Office, 214, 215, 216, 233, 244
Inkerman, battle of (1854), 79, 84
Inkerman Café, 128, 129
International Congress of Hygiene and Demography, London, 241
International Statistical Congress, London, 186
Introductory Notes on Lying-in Institutions (FN), 220
Institution for the Care of Sick Gentlewomen, 1, Harley Street, 47–55, 59
Ipsamboul, 41
Italy, Nightingale family travels in, 11, 16–17

Jones, Agnes, 217–18, 221
Jowett, Benjamin, 222–3, 229–30, 245, 247; on FN's religious writings, 194, 227–8; friendship with FN, 195, 223, 240; death, 243
Jura, 124

Kaiserswerth, Institution of Deaconesses, 29, 40, 43, 59, 217; FN visits, 42, 44–6; writes pamphlet on, 42
Kalamita Bay, 59, 62
Karnak, 41

Khartoum, 238
Kensington Borough, mortality in, 160
King's College Hospital, 59, 238
Kinglake, Alexander, 70
Kingsley, Charles, 194
Koch, Dr, 238
Koulali Hospital, 89, 132

Lambeth, 186
Landor, Walter Savage, 27
Lansdowne, Lord, 131
Lawfield, Mrs, 81
Lawrence, Sir John, 211, 222, 243, 247;
    Viceroy of India, 212–8, 214; death,
    229
Lea Hurst, Derbyshire, 14, 15, 20, 223;
    FN's love of, 24, 34; Mrs Gaskell at,
    55, 58; FN returns from Crimea to,
    147, 150; transfer of Nightingale
    family to, 227
Lefroy, Colonel John, 140–1, 150, 153
Leopold, King of the Belgians, 178
Lepsius, Karl Richard, 23
Lewis, Sir George, 175, 196
Liddell, Sir John, 163
Life of the Prince Consort, The, 230
Life or Death in India (FN), 229
Lisbon, 184
Lister, Joseph, 30, 187
Liverpool, 216
Longfellow, Henry Wadsworth, 88
Louis Napoleon, 17
Lyons, 184

MacDonald, Mr, 75, 79, 84
McGrigor, Dr, 98, 99, 133
McNeill, Lady, 168
McNeill, Sir John, 166, 237; in Crimean
    campaign, 110–13, 120, 140; and
    army medical reform, 151, 153, 160;
    report on Commissariat, 156, 157;
    death, 240
Madras, 203
Maison de la Providence, 47
Malta, 209, 211
Malvern, 40, 166
Manning, Cardinal, 46, 72, 75, 84

Marseilles, 75
Martin, Dr, 166, 198
Martineau, Harriet, 178, 198, 201
Mayo, Lord, 222
Melbourne, Lord, 20–1
Memoires (Mme Roland), 211
Menzies, Dr, 71, 76, 98
Metropolitan Workhouse Infirmary Act,
    218, 221
Michelangelo, 34
Middlesex Hospital, 55
Mill, J. S., 194
Milnes, Richard Monckton (Lord
    Houghton), 75, 106, 131, 247;
    character and appearance, 27; turned
    down by FN, 40–1; death, 240
Mohl, Julius, 186, 208; marries Mary
    Clarke, 40; death, 227
Mohl, Mary, 46, 53, 72, 163, 237;
    character and appearance, 17–21;
    FN's correspondence with, 27, 166,
    195, 197, 210, 217; marriage, 40;
    FN stays with, 47; FN refuses to see,
    209; death, 240
Moore, Thomas, 27
Mortality in the British Army (FN), 171

Napier, Lord Francis, 222
Napier of Magdala, Lord Robert, 222
National Society for Aid to the Sick and
    Wounded (later British Red Cross),
    224
Netley General Military Hospital, 153,
    157–9, 184
Newcastle, Duke of, 64–5, 71, 164
New South Wales, 221
Nicholson family, 14–15, 20, 23
Nicholson, Hannah, 24, 38
Nicholson, Henry, 21, 27
Nicholson, Marianne, 20, 21, 171, 195
Nightingale, Fanny, 41, 71, 120, 166;
    early travels, 11; character, 14; and
    Parthe, 15, 46; and FN, 20, 23, 38, 56,
    174, 211, 223; attitude to FN's work,
    29–30, 40, 42–6, 47, 75, 163–4; old
    age, 214, 223, 227; death, 230

Nightingale, Florence
    early years: family background, 10;
    birth, 11; early efforts to realize
    ambition, 10, 16, 29, 38, 40; diary and
    intimate scribblings, 10, 17, 34, 43,
    228; education, 15, 21–3; habit of
    'dreaming', 15, 24, 34, 38, 41, 42, 43;
    relations with Parthe, 15, 43, 46, 47,
    163, 165, 166, 211, 230; social life,
    16, 17–20, 21–4, 38; religious life,
    16, 21, 27, 34, 41, 43, 192–5, 227–30;
    sense of mission, 16, 21, 27, 41; use of
    statistics, 17, 160, 185–6, 199, 201–2,
    219; appearance, 20, 138, 140, 243;
    and Henry Nicholson, 21; emotional
    life, 21, 30–4, 40, 43, 132, 195–6;
    relations with parents, 24, 29, 40, 41,
    43, 44–7, 56, 71, 75, 163–4, 166, 168,
    211, 223; and Milnes, 27, 40–1;
    health, 34, 124, 132, 133, 163, 165–6,
    173–4, 197, 211, 240; visit to Rome,
    34–5; meets Sidney Herbert, 35;
    collaboration with Herbert, *see*
    Herbert, Sidney; mastery of
    documentation, 40, 159–63, 199–202;
    pets, 42, 58, 195, 196, 210, 211;
    writings: on Kaiserswerth, 42; on
    health in army, 160, 171, 198;
    memoir on Herbert, 182; on hospital
    design, 184; on nursing, 188–91; on
    religion, 192–5, 228; on health in
    India, 199–200, 229, 236, 241; on
    childbirth, 220; on poor law, 223;
    remarks on women, women's rights, etc:
    46; 166, 190–1, 220; first appointment,
    47–59; as a nurse, 53; character and
    attributes, 56, 246–7;
    in Crimean War: 70–147; at
    Scutari, 70, 76–117, 124–32, 133;
    relations with doctors, 76, 77, 79–81,
    92, 98; management of nurses, 77,
    81–3, 99, 107, 109, 117, 133, 138–40,
    142, 146; and Dr Hall, 98, 120, 131,
    132, 141; and soldiers, 88, 89, 106–7,
    124, 128, 129–31, 146, 208; at
    Balaclava, 117, 120–4, 133, 142;
    popular feeling for, 131, 132, 146, 156,

182–3, 244; returns to England, 146–7, 150;
after Crimean War: and army medical reforms, 150–75; will, 168, 245; advocacy of preventive medicine, 160, 172; and hospital reform, 183–7; and nurses' training, 188–92, 220–3, 224–7; devotion to Herbert, 182, 195, 196, 202, 245; and Canadian expedition, 196–8; and India, 198–203, 211, 214–16, 222–3, 224, 229, 241; retreats from contact with friends, 209; establishment at 35 South Street, 211, 230–3; and mortality in childbirth, 219–20; receives Royal Red Cross, 236; old age, 243–5; receives OM, 244–5; death, 245–6

Nightingale, Parthenope, 23, 24, 44, 46, 147, 174; relations with FN, *see* Nightingale, Florence; early life, 14, 15, 16–20; health, 44, 241; on FN, 53, 56, 150, 195; and FN's work, 129, 163; marriage, 168; death, 241

Nightingale, William Edward, 71, 178, 194; travels, 11, 16–17; character, 14; estates, 14–15; educates daughters, 15, 24; attitude to FN, 43, 163, 211; death, 227

Nightingale Fund, 128–9, 188, 191, 192

Nightingale Training School for Nurses, St Thomas' Hospital, 191, 220–2, 224–7

Nineteenth Century, 229

Northcote, Sir Stafford, 214, 215–16

Norwood, 72, 209

Note on Pauperism, A (FN), 223

Notes on the British Army (FN), 160, 171, 198

Notes on Hospitals (FN), 184

Notes on Nursing (FN), 188–91

Observations on the Sanitary State of the Army in India (FN), 199–200

Osborne, Rev. Sidney Godolphin, 81, 84

Osburn, Lucy, 221

Paget, Sir James, 192

Palmerston, Lord, 171, 172, 175; friendship with Nightingales, 23; supports FN, 109, 117, 129; and Netley Hospital, 157–9

Panmure, Lord, Earl of Dalhousie: and Crimean War, 109–10, 117, 129, 140, 146; and army medical reform, 150, 151–3, 154–9, 164–5, 171

Paris, 184, 186; FN visits, 17–20, 47; Sisters of Charity, 46, 47

Pasteur, Louis, 30

Paulet, Lord William, 99, 128

Pedro V of Portugal, 184

Peel, Sir Robert, 35

Pembroke, Earl of, 35

Peninsula War (1808–14), 92

Poor Law Bill, 218

Poor Law Board, 218

Pringle, Angelique, 226

Prussia, Crown Princess of, 224

Quetelet, Adolphe, 186

Quinet, Edgar, 194

Raglan, Lord (Lord Fitzroy Somerset), 117, 124, 132

Rathbone, William, 216, 217

Recamier, Mme Julie, 17, 20

Red Cross, 224

Rev. Mother of the Bermondsey nuns, 132, 143

Ring and the Book, The, 233

Ripon, Lord, *see* de Grey, Lord

Robert Lowe, 120

Roberts, Lord, 233, 245

Roberts, Mrs, 81, 120, 124, 132, 133

Roebuck, Mr, 109

Roland, Mme Manon, 211

Rome, 184; FN visits, 34–5

Royal College of Surgeons, 191

Royal Commission on the Sanitary Condition of the Army, 151, 153–65; sub-Commissions, 165

Royal Commission (on health of army in India), 198–201

Russell, William Howard, 59, 62, 84, 131, 154

St Bartholomew's Hospital, 192

St John's House, Blandford Square, 72, 83

St Pancras parish, mortality in, 160

St Thomas' Hospital, 143; rebuilding, 184–6; nurses' training at 188–92, 224–7, 241; nurses sent out from, 217

Salisbury, Lord, 229

Salisbury, Miss, 138–40

Salisbury Infirmary, 29

Sanitary Commission to Crimea, 109–10

Scutari, 63, 70, 76–117, 104; Barrack Hospital, 63–4, 76, 80, 128, 146; conditions in, 76–7, 79, 81, 98, 110; catering arrangements at, 77–9, 89, 101, 113–17; General Hospital, 80; cemetary, 106; cholera, 106, 133; Sanitary Commission, 110; recreation for soldiers at, 128–31

Sebastopol, 59, 62, 121, 132

Sellonite sisters, 72, 76, 104

Shaftesbury, Lord, 23, 110

Shakespeare, William, 190

Shaw Stewart, Miss, 109, 132, 133, 143

Shore, William Edward, *see* Nightingale, William Edward

Sillery, Major, 76

Simpson, Sir James Young, 187

Sisters of Charity, Paris, 46, 47; in Crimean War, 64

Sistine Chapel, 34

Smith, Adam, 23

Smith, Dr Andrew, 75, 92, 109, 132, 154; and Royal Commission, 154, 159

Smith, Mai (FN's aunt), 161, 247; and FN's education, 21–3; correspondence of FN with, 132; in Crimean War, 133–8, 146; assists FN in England, 164, 166, 168, 171; 'defection', 183, 196

Smith, Octavius (FN's uncle), 23

Smith, Sam (FN's uncle), 21, 75, 128; 'business manager', 182, 183

Smith, Samuel (great-grandfather), 14

Smith, Shore, 21, 243
Smith, William, 14
Social Science Congress, Liverpool, 184
Somerset, Lord Fitzroy, *see* Raglan, Lord
South, Mr J. F., 191–2
South-Eastern Railway, 184
South Street, FN at no. 32, 195; 'Little India Office', 208; at no. 35, 211, 230–3
Soyer, M Alexis; in Crimean War, 113–14, 120–1, 124, 132, 143; in England, 171–2, 179
Spa, Belgium, 175, 178
Stanley, Lord (15th Earl of Derby), 198, 203
Stanley, Mary, 72; in Crimea, 83, 84, 88, 89, 109, 117; breach with FN, 140
Stanmore, Lord, 172
Storks, General Henry, 128, 146, 166
Strachey, John, 223
Strachey, Lytton, 178
Stratford de Redcliffe, Lady, 71, 98, 99, 117, 140
Stratford de Redcliffe, Lord, 71, 84, 98, 117, 140
Strelecki, Count, 175
Suggestions for Thought (FN), 194
Sutherland, Dr John, 110, 216, 247; collaboration with FN, 153, 161, 196, 198–9, 216, 238; relations with FN, 164, 165–6, 207–8, 208–9, 238, 240; goes to Gibraltar and Malta, 211; death, 240–1
Sutherland, Mrs, 210
Sydney Infirmary, 221

Taylor, Fanny, 89
Tennyson, Alfred, 27
Thackeray, William M., 27
Thatcher, Temperance, 230
Therapia, 84
Times, The, 24, 218; Crimean despatches, 59, 62, 64, 84; fund, 64, 75, 79, 84, 98
Tocqueville, Alexis de, 27
Torrance, Elizabeth, 221
Tulloch, Colonel Alexander, R. E., 166; in Crimea, 113, 120, 140; and army medical reform, 151, 153; reports on Commissariat, 156, 157

Varna, 59, 62, 98
Vectis, 75–6
Verney, Frederick, 241
Verney, Sir Harry, 168, 195, 230, 241, 245, 247; as MP, 218; death, 243
Victoria, Queen, 156, 159; and Lord Melbourne, 20–1; and soldiers in the Crimea, 104, 106, 129; and FN, 106 129, 151–3, 230, 136–8; and army medical reform, 159, 171; and Indian Sanitary Commission, 198, 199–200
Victoria School of Nursing, Berlin, 224
Villa Colombaia, 11
Villiers, Charles, 218

Wadi Halfa, 238, 240
Wantage, Lady, 244
Wantage, Lord, 236

Ward, Lord, 124
Wardroper, Mrs, 188, 192, 222, 227
War Office: antagonism to FN at, 132, 138, 141, 154, 172–3; Herbert at, 172–5
Waverley Abbey, Farnham, 14, 20
Weare, Miss, 117
Wellington, Duke of, 117, 129
Wellington Barracks, 172
West Indies, 208
West Wellow, 29
Whitfield, Dr, 184–5, 192
Whybron, Trooper Thomas, 129
Williams, Rachel, 227, 230, 238
Wilton House, Wiltshire, 35, 178
Winchester Infirmary, 184
Winkworth, Emily and Catherine, 56
Wolseley, Lord, 236
Woodham-Smith, Mrs Cecil, 164
Woolwich: arsenal, 172; military hospital, 175
Workhouse Infirmary, Liverpool, 216–18
Workhouse Infirmary Act, *see* Metropolitan Workhouse Infirmary Act
Wreford, Mr, 101

Yarmouth, 173
Yule, Colonel, 241

Zemindar, the Sun and the Watering Pot as Affecting Life or Death in India, The (FN), 229–30